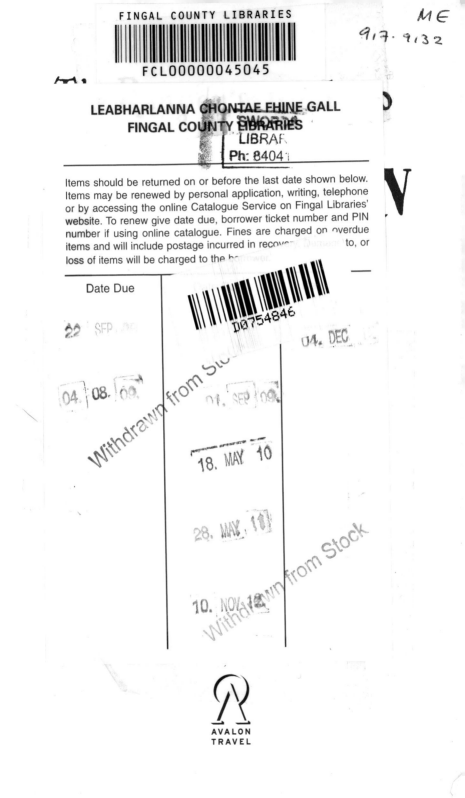

LEABHARLANNA CHONTAE FHINE GALL
FINGAL COUNTY LIBRARIES
LIBRARY
Ph: 8404

Items should be returned on or before the last date shown below. Items may be renewed by personal application, writing, telephone or by accessing the online Catalogue Service on Fingal Libraries' website. To renew give date due, borrower ticket number and PIN number if using online catalogue. Fines are charged on overdue items and will include postage incurred in recovery. Damage to, or loss of items will be charged to the borrower.

Date Due		
22 SEP		04. DEC
04. 08. 00	04. SEP 09	
	18. MAY 10	
	28. MAY 10	
	10. NOV	

AVALON
TRAVEL

The Ranger's Guide to the Grand Canyon
1st Edition

Avalon Travel
a member of the Perseus Books Group
1700 Fourth Street
Berkeley, CA 94710, USA
atpfeedback@avalonpub.com
www.avalontravelbooks.com

Editors: Grace Fujimoto, Michelle Cadden
Graphics Coordinator: Stefano Boni
Production Coordinator: Darren Alessi
Cover Designer: Darren Alessi
Indexer: Judy Hunt

ISBN-10: 1-59880-128-7
ISBN-13: 978-1-59880-128-6
ISSN: 1941-4587

Printing History
1st Edition — June 2008
5 4 3 2 1

Although every effort was made to ensure that the information was correct at the time of
going to press, the author and publisher do not assume and hereby disclaim any liability to
any party for any loss or damage caused by errors, omissions, or any potential travel disrup-
tion due to labor or financial difficulty, whether such errors or omissions result from negli-
gence, accident, or any other cause.

Contents

·Foreword·

Many visitors arrive at the Grand Canyon with little information about the area or what they're about to see. This was true for our family of six when we first arrived at the Grand Canyon in 1975 with our worldly possessions packed in a moving van. We arrived without reservations or overnight arrangements during one of the busiest times of year—the week between Christmas and New Year's—never imagining that this would be our home for the next 15 years and that our four children would all graduate from Grand Canyon High School. Like many others, our expectations were no match for the first glimpse of the canyon. I still marvel at the reactions of visitors who are standing on the rim for the first time, looking as though they are gazing out on the last frontier. The canyon continues to have the same influence on people from diverse cultures around the world.

As I look back, I can trace how this place has grown and changed, both in legend and in popularity. If you wrote to the park in 1933, you would have received a 54-page booklet with maps and photos describing every aspect of your visit. The same letter written in 1999 might produce brochures containing general information about the park. Each year, 70 percent of Grand Canyon visitors arrive for their first and last visit. Other travelers return again and again to explore every inch of the area. This book is designed to help all visitors gather information, and glean some insider knowledge of this amazing place.

Another change is in the ranks of rangers that run the park. In 1933, visitors would have taken a guided walk with one of only three ranger-naturalists, who were all permanent national park service employees assigned to the Grand Canyon. Evening campfire programs were special events that often featured a prominent visiting college professor who gave programs on the history of the area. Today, most programs are given by seasonal rangers, often called park interpreters, who help make your trip truly special. Visitors are often surprised to learn that these employees return yearly, just for the reward of living and working in a national park. They spend many hours developing interesting walks, talks, and other programs without paid vacations and other benefits associated with permanent park employees. They certainly made my tenure at the Grand Canyon easier. In appreciation for the work of these unsung heroes of the National Park system, this book is dedicated to the many seasonal rangers who make the experience of visiting the Grand Canyon worthwhile for so many.

Jack O'Brien
Cottonwood, Arizona
February 15, 2008

· Introduction ·

Grand Canyon National Park and the surrounding national forests and recreational area offer an amazing array of natural wonders, activities, accommodations, and facilities. Before you begin your adventure there, you'll probably want to ask a few questions about what to do, and when and how to do those things. This book offers you a quick and easy way of finding the answers you need. Your guide through the book will be Ranger Jack—who closely resembles former Ranger Jack O'Brien, who was Chief of Interpretation at Grand Canyon for many years. He's been around long enough to have heard all the questions that visitors ask, and to know the answers. We thought he would be a natural to guide you through the canyon as only an insider can.

The question-and-answer format we use originally came from "100+ Common Visitor Questions & Answers," a document that the National Park Service Division of Interpretation at Yosemite national Park created to help park rangers and interpretive staff get quickly oriented.

We've updated many of those questions, provided answers specific to the Grand Canyon, and added lots of others to help you learn some inside information about this magnificent park and its surroundings. We hope this Ranger's Guide will add to your enjoyment of the Grand Canyon, whatever your interests and however long your visit.

I
Getting there

Where is the Grand Canyon?

Chiseled along 277 miles of the Colorado River in northern Arizona, Grand Canyon National Park includes more than 1,217,403 acres of forests, streams, waterfalls, alpine meadows, deserts, canyons, and plateaus. It encompasses five of North America's seven life zones and three of its four deserts. More than 500 miles of hiking trails traverse the park's three geographically distinct areas: the South Rim, the North Rim, and the Inner Canyon. The mighty Colorado River provides one of the world's longest stretches of navigable white water, dividing the park's North and South Rims. The Grand Canyon's varied terrain is home to 1,737 flowering plants, 373 bird species, 91 species of mammals, 17 kinds of fish, 57 species of reptiles and amphibians, an unknown number of insects, and some of the most awesome scenery you'll ever see.

Here are some road mileage figures to Grand Canyon National Park:

Via Interstate 40 from the west:

- From Williams, Arizona   59 miles
- From Ash Fork, Arizona   78 miles
- From Seligman, Arizona   101 miles
- From Kingman, Arizona   171 miles
- From Hoover Dam   242 miles
- From Las Vegas, Nevada   273 miles
- From Los Angeles, California   507 miles
- From San Francisco, California 820 miles

Via Interstate 40 from the east:

- From Flagstaff, Arizona   92 miles
- From Winslow, Arizona   150 miles
- From Gallup, New Mexico   280 miles
- From Albuquerque, New Mexico   415 miles

Leabharlanna Fhine Gall

- From Santa Fe, New Mexico   477 miles
- From Denver, Colorado   879 miles
- From St. Louis, Missouri   1,499 miles

Via Interstate 17 from the south:
- From Phoenix, Arizona   247 miles
- From Tucson, Arizona   334 miles

Via Highway 89 from the north:
- From Zion National Park   272 miles
- From Bryce Canyon National Park   310 miles
- From Salt Lake City, Utah   594 miles

How do we get there?

Depending upon your time and budget, you can get to the Grand Canyon by car, plane, bus, shuttle, or train.

SOUTH RIM

By Car

You can enter the park at the south entrance station from Highway 64. From Williams or Flagstaff, Highway 64 can be reached by Interstate 40. From Williams, the south entrance to the park is 63 miles on a fairly straight but hilly two-lane road that runs through a landscape of sagebrush and desert scrub, broken up by ponderosa and pinyon-juniper forests. This route offers little in the way of gas stations, campgrounds, restaurants, or other accommodations, but that doesn't deter a steady stream of auto, bus, and RV traffic. In the winter months, the road might be icy and occasionally snowpacked, so call for recorded road conditions (928/638-7888) before you leave Williams. Drivers should also watch for elk and deer that often dart across the road as it winds through the ponderosa forests. Two miles outside the park, the road passes through the community of Tusayan, where visitor services can be found, including lodging, camping, food, and fuel. Once you're in the park, you'll drive or shuttle on a two-lane road to the South Rim, the Visitor Center at Canyon View Information Plaza (accessible only by shuttle), and Grand Canyon Village, where most of the park's facilities and services are located.

From Flagstaff, you can follow Highway 180 west to Highway 64, and then drive another 28 miles to the park's south entrance. Highway 180 is also a two-lane road, but with many more curves and hills than the road from Williams. No services are available between Flagstaff and the Highway 64 junction, but again, traffic is usually heavy. Call for road conditions (928/638-7888) before you leave Flagstaff, as winter storms occasionally close the road, and icy conditions are common. This route travels along a striking volcanic landscape; be sure to keep an eye out for the Red Butte, an erosion remnant a few miles north of the Highway 180/64 junction, and Humphreys Peak, the highest point in Arizona at 12,643 feet.

If you're driving from the east, Highway 89 joins with Highway 64 near Cameron, Arizona, on the Navajo Indian Reservation. You'll find gas stations and limited food services in and around Cameron, which will provide the only services or facilities until you reach Desert View, which is 30 miles away at the east park entrance and where you'll find limited services and seasonal gas. This route follows another two-lane hilly road, with heavy traffic that takes you through desert scrub and pinyon-juniper forests. In the winter, call for road conditions (928/638-7888) before you travel.

By Air

You can fly to the nearest airports at Flagstaff, Arizona (80 miles southeast); Phoenix, Arizona (220 miles south); and Las Vegas, Nevada (220 miles west, 928/638-2446). There is limited air service to the smaller Grand Canyon Airport (10 miles south of the park). Major car rental agencies serve the Phoenix, Flagstaff, and Las Vegas airports, but car rentals are no longer available at the Grand Canyon Airport. Shuttle service between Phoenix and Flagstaff and between Flagstaff and the Grand Canyon Village can be arranged through Open Road Tours (800/766-7117) and Flagstaff Express Shuttle (800/563-1980).

By Bus

Greyhound Bus Lines (Flagstaff office 928/774-4573 or 800/231-2222) provides scheduled service to Flagstaff and Williams, Arizona from points nationwide. Trips between Phoenix and Flagstaff and between Flagstaff,

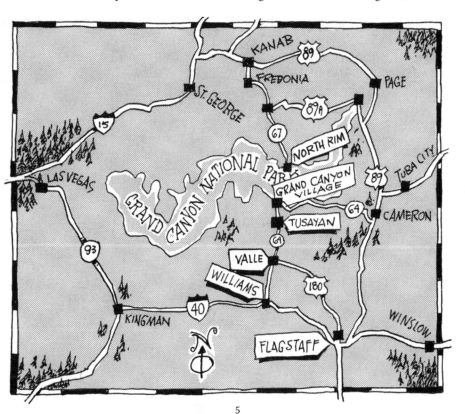

Williams, and the Grand Canyon Village can be made through Open Road Tours (928/226-8060 or 877/226-8060) or through Flagstaff Express Shuttle services (928/225-2290 or 800/563-1980).

By Train
AMTRAK (800/872-7245, www.amtrak.com) provides scheduled service to Flagstaff, Arizona from points nationwide. The Grand Canyon Railway (800/843-8724, www.thetrain.com) runs historic excursion trains from Williams, Arizona, to the canyon daily except for December 24 and 25. These trains offer five classes of service departing Williams as early as 9 A.M. and arriving at the Grand Canyon at 11:15 A.M. For the return, trains depart at 3 P.M. and arrive back in Williams at 5:15 P.M. Prices range $65–170 for adults, $40–145 for youth 11–16, and $30–95 for children 2–10. Prices depend on the level of class and are subject to change. Overnight packages are available.

NORTH RIM

By Car
From the north, you can reach the Grand Canyon from Las Vegas and Salt Lake City along Interstate 15. You then take Highway 389 to Fredonia, Highway 89A to Jacob Lake, and Highway 67 to the north entrance of the park. This route runs through canyon and plateau lands and boasts such attractions as the Kaibab Paiute Indian Reservation and Pipe Spring National Monument. But there are limited services and facilities along the way.

By Air, Bus, or Train
The nearest major cities are Salt Lake City, Utah (380 miles north) and Las Vegas, Nevada (280 miles southwest). Regularly scheduled airlines, buses, and trains serve both cities. From there, you'll have to rent a car, as there is no regular air, bus, or train service directly to the North Rim.

TRANS-CANYON SHUTTLE
Daily round-trip shuttle service (928/638-2820) between the South and North Rims is provided mid-May–mid-October. It departs North Rim at 7 A.M. and reaches South Rim at 11:30 A.M. then departs South Rim at 1:30 P.M. and arrives at North Rim at 6 P.M. Fare per person is $70 one-way, $130 round-trip. Reservations are required. Call the service directly, or contact one of the lodging transportation desks.

How much does it cost to get in?

Considering that you're paying to see one of the Seven Natural Wonders of the World and one of the most beautiful and dramatic landscapes you'll ever see, it's a real bargain.

As you enter one of three park gates, you'll pay an entrance fee that's good for seven days for both Rims. A ranger will give you a map of the park with basic park information, an admission receipt, and a free copy of *The Guide*—the park newspaper with up-to-date listings and schedules for all park activities, including information on parking areas, shuttle bus routes, ranger programs and more. Remember to keep your admission receipt to re-enter the park if you leave it or drive between the North and South Rims. If you're lucky enough to arrive on August 25, you won't have to pay any entrance fee, because we waive the cost on that day to honor the founding of the National Park Service. Educational fee waivers are administered by the Fee Management Office (928/638-7850). Applications must be received 4–6 weeks in advance of the anticipated visit.

Private non-commercial vehicles.................................... $25
(valid for seven days, both rims)

Individuals arriving by bus, foot, bicycle, horse, or skis................. $15
(valid for seven days, both rims)

Annual Pass $50
(valid for one year from date of purchase, both rims)

America the Beautiful—Annual Pass............................... $80
(good for all National Parks for one year from date of purchase)

America the Beautiful—Senior Pass................................ $10
(a lifetime pass to all National Parks for
U.S. citizens or permanent residents who are 62 and older)

America the Beautiful—Access Pass............................... Free
(for blind or permanently disabled U.S. citizens or permanent residents)

> When's the best time of year to See the Grand Canyon?

Speaking from experience, I can say that any season in the Grand Canyon has its rewards. It just depends on what part of the park you visit, and what you want to see and do. My favorite times are October, with its temperate weather and fewer crowds, and the often-crowded December holidays, when the canyon may be magically clad in snow.

South Rim

The South Rim, open year-round, is the most accessible area of the park by all modes of transportation. It also has the most visitors, facilities, and services. Most visitors arrive April–September, and the least November–February. There is an average annual precipitation of about 16 inches. Spring usually arrives late in the high country of the South Rim (elevation 7,100 feet), with lots of unpredictable weather. March and April often combine winter and spring conditions, while May and June are traditionally the driest months. Summer arrives suddenly in June with dependably hot temperatures, large crowds, and monsoon rains in the afternoons. Summer nighttime temperatures are generally cool. Fall comes by mid-September, casting its golden light on the canyon walls and offering temperatures that range between the high 30s (Fahrenheit) at night to the 60s during the day. You can usually expect a dusting of snow by Halloween and a major snowstorm by Thanksgiving. Winter on the South Rim (November–February) can be very cold, with below-zero temperatures at night and up to 50–100 inches of snow per year. But in any season, the weather here is erratic. Snow can fall and melt within a few days or stay on the ground all winter, or it can become a deluge of rain in December.

Inner Canyon

While ice and snow may remain on the rims, visitors who venture down below the South Rim into the Inner Canyon can enjoy the soothing desert warmth and colorful wildflowers as early as March. A mile below the North and South Rims, the Colorado River at Phantom Ranch is still 2,400 feet above sea level.

Year-round, the weather here is drier and hotter than anywhere else in the park, with summer highs well over 100°F. Rain and snow are scarce here, with a mere nine inches of rain per year.

North Rim

This is the coolest and wettest part of the park, with about 26 inches of precipitation a year. During the visitor season, mid-May–mid-October, warm clothing and bedding are a necessity. Early in the spring at Jacob Lake, snowplows start to clear the entrance road to the park, completing the job about one month later. The North Rim opens in mid-May, usually with snow still on the ground. The rainy season runs mid-July–mid-August, when afternoon thunderstorms may bring downpours, flash flooding, trail washouts, and lightning. As early as September, the snow begins to fall, with heavy winter weather closing the North Rim to visitors in November or early December. More than 10 feet of snow will accumulate during the winter season on the North Rim.

You can enjoy any time of year at the Grand Canyon. Just keep in mind that desert and near-desert areas have no "average" seasons. Year-round, the only predictable element is the extreme and dramatic weather that makes this place one of the most scenic areas in the world.

Is the park always open to visitors?

Although the park is open 24 hours a day, 365 days a year, the roads are not. Winter snows, freezing temperatures, and dangerous driving conditions close the entrance road into the North Rim, making that area of the park unreachable by most visitors. That doesn't mean that the more adventuresome can't ski or snowshoe into the North Rim, as long as they can negotiate deep snow and cold temperatures. The state of Arizona closes the entrance road to the North Rim to vehicles on the first big snowfall, which usually occurs in early December. The entrance station closes October 15, and the Backcountry Office closes October 31. The North Rim entrance reopens to visitors in cars and buses on May 15, after the spring thaw.

Spring in the Grand Canyon often brings flash floods and rockslides that may cause certain areas of the park and hiking trails to close to visitors. On the North Rim, early spring is the time when we usually close small portions of the North Kaibab Trail for maintenance and repair from winter damage. Visitors arriving in cars can drive into the Grand Canyon Lodge, but not to Cape Royal and Point Imperial, because it takes longer to open these higher-elevation roads, which usually get more snow. In the early spring and late fall, the North Rim is usually open for day-use only before snow closes the roads. Call the North Rim Visitor Center (928/638-7864) for more information. A 24-hour recorded information line (928/638-7888) is available for park and road conditions.

It's not always Mother Nature's fault; sometimes it's just plain human nature that makes the park inaccessible. For the first time in the park's history, the Grand Canyon was closed to visitors in 1995 and 1996 because of a government shutdown over budget negotiations.

What services are available?

Most of the park's visitor services are found along the South Rim of the Grand Canyon, but you'll be able to find seasonal services along the North Rim and limited year-round services in the Inner Canyon.

South Rim

Along the South Rim and in Tusayan (just outside the south entrance), you'll find the following services:

- A full range of lodging choices at the El Tovar Hotel, Kachina Lodge, Thunderbird Lodge, Bright Angel Lodge, Maswik Lodge, Yavapai Lodge, Moqui Lodge, Trailer Village, and numerous other motel lodgings

- Several campgrounds inside the park and in Tusayan, including one RV campground (with hookups) and three backcountry campgrounds

- Grand Canyon Association bookstores located at the Yavapai Observation Station, Kolb Studio, Canyon View Information Plaza, and in the Tusayan Museum

- Year-round and seasonal dining facilities, including the Arizona Room, the dining room at the El Tovar Hotel, a coffee shop at the Bright Angel Lodge, a snack bar at the Desert View Trading Post, and cafeterias at Maswik and Yavapai Lodges

- Three general stores: one in Grand Canyon Village Marketplace called the General Store at Market Plaza with groceries, camping equipment, digital photo printing, and more. A second general store is located in Tusayan, and a third is located in Desert View.

11

- A vast array of gift, book, and curio shops located in most lodgings, as well as in the Hopi House, Verkamp's Curios, Hermits Rest Gift Shop, Desert View Trading Post, and Lookout Studio
- A ranger station, backcountry permit office, and National Park Service administrative offices
- An amphitheater
- A train depot
- A shuttle service
- Coin-operated shower and laundry facilities next to Mather Campground
- A medical clinic and pharmacy
- A Chase bank and an ATM Machine
- A post office
- Several churches and numerous interdenominational worship services
- A garage with towing services in Grand Canyon Village and gas in Tusayan
- Childcare services
- K-12 public schools
- Kennels

North Rim

Visitor services on the North Rim are only available mid-May–late October. Once overnight accommodations close for the season, there are no food, lodging, or fuel services to be found anywhere along the North Rim. During the summer and fall, the following services are available:

- Lodging at the Grand Canyon Lodge
- Gift shop in the Grand Canyon Lodge
- An amphitheater
- One developed campground with tent and RV sites (no hookups)
- Coin-operated shower and laundry facilities
- A trans-canyon shuttle
- An NPS visitor center, a ranger station, and a backcountry office
- A Grand Canyon Association bookstore in the visitor center
- Dining facilities in the Grand Canyon Lodge complex, including a dining room, saloon, and deli
- A service station for fuel and minor auto repairs

- A grocery and general store in campground
- A post office
- Interdenominational worship services

Inner Canyon

The only way to get to the Inner Canyon is by foot, mule, or horse on one of the many canyon trails. The only lodging and meal service facility below either rim is located at Phantom Ranch near the Colorado River. The Inner Canyon has three developed campgrounds: Indian Garden below the South Rim, Bright Angel near Phantom Ranch, and Cottonwood below the North Rim. Toilets are located in several places along the trails into the canyon.

Who runs the Grand Canyon?

Although the park belongs to all of us, the U.S. National Park Service (NPS), which is part of the Department of the Interior, makes the rules in Grand Canyon National Park. This means you won't see any highway patrol officers, sheriffs, or municipal firefighters during your visit. Look instead for a park ranger if you need a helping hand.

The NPS has plenty of people around who make sure things run smoothly. Park rangers handle law enforcement, traffic regulation, search and rescue, and other duties. Park naturalists and interpreters (who are also park rangers) provide all the educational walks, talks, and programs in the park. The people dressed in green pants, gray shirts, and dark green baseball caps are the park maintenance, fire, and resource management workers. All of us report to the NPS administrators like the superintendent and chief ranger.

The Grand Canyon Association (GCA) is a nonprofit group that operates bookstores throughout the park and publishes informational and interpretive materials in support of park programs. Supported by membership fees and donations, it also provides funds for exhibits, preservation of historic park buildings and artifacts, and development of scientific knowledge of the Grand Canyon area. Since its founding in 1932, the GCA (formerly the Grand Canyon Natural History Association) has donated over $20 million to the Grand Canyon National Park since 1932. The GCA, together with the NPS, cosponsors the Grand Canyon Field Institute. This nonprofit school offers a wide range of short field courses and nature study opportunities in the park March–November.

To help with many park services, the NPS has contracted with private concession companies, but the NPS authorizes prices and service rates. Xanterra operates Grand Canyon National Park Lodges and provided many park services, including lodging, food services, retail stores, service stations, interpretive sightseeing tours, and other visitor services. Delaware North Park Services operates two general stores inside the park, and Verkamp's operates the oldest gift, book, and curio store on the South Rim.

The Grand Canyon National Park Foundation is a nonprofit organization that raises money to support projects and programs approved by the NPS, including restoration, preservation, and wildlife protection in the park. The foundation is funded by corporations, foundations, and individuals interested in helping the park.

The Grand Canyon Trust is a nonprofit organization that promotes the conservation of natural resources of the Colorado Plateau. Based in Flagstaff, Arizona, the trust has successfully lobbied for regional and national legislation that helps protect the park.

You can contact the NPS, Grand Canyon concession companies, and other organizations at the following addresses or numbers:

National Park Service
P.O. Box 129
Grand Canyon, AZ 86023
928/638-7888
www.nps.gov/grca

Grand Canyon Association
P.O. Box 399
Grand Canyon, AZ 86023
928/638-2481 or 800/858-2808
www.grandcanyon.org

Xanterra Parks and Resorts (Reservations)
6312 South Fiddlers Green Cir., Suite 600N
Greenwood Village, CO 80111
928/638-2631 (same day reservations),
303/297-2757, or 888/297-2757
www.grandcanyonlodges.com

Grand Canyon Field Institute
P.O. Box 399
Grand Canyon, AZ 86023
928/638-2485 or 866/471-4435
www.grandcanyon.org/fieldinstitute

The Grand Canyon National Park Foundation
625 N. Beaver St.
Flagstaff, AZ 86001
928/774-1760
www.grandcanyonfoundation.org

Grand Canyon Trust
2601 N. Fort Valley Rd.
Flagstaff, AZ 86001
928/774-7488 or 888/GCT-5550
www.grandcanyontrust.org

What you bring depends on where you stay and what you do in the park, but I can name some basic items that will make your trip more comfortable. For advice on special activities like camping and hiking, turn to the *Camping and Backpacking* and *Recreational Opportunities* chapters.

From spring through fall, our weather is hard to predict. Storms can appear suddenly, bringing rain, wind, and really cold temperatures. Summers are hot and dry on the South Rim, but afternoon thunderstorms can bring sudden temperature drops. If you're in the Inner Canyon, expect scorching summer temperatures, both day and night. My advice to all visitors: Be prepared for these abrupt changes. And, whatever the season, dress in layers that you can add or subtract.

The park has three distinct temperature zones. The bottom of the Inner Canyon has an elevation of about 2,400 feet, which means summertime temperatures can exceed 110°F. The elevation on the North Rim exceeds 9,000 feet and on the South Rim it exceeds 7,000 feet. Expect summer temperatures on the rims to be in the 70s and 80s, with chilly nights (even in midsummer). The ultraviolet radiation is intense, so sunscreen, sunglasses, and hats are a must. The high elevation, high temperatures, and extra activity can become a problem for those visitors with breathing or heart ailments. It's best to check with your physician about special precautions you can take to help prevent heart attacks and respiratory failure.

Winter arrives quickly in the park, and if you're not prepared, it can be downright dangerous. Some years our first snowfall comes in October, so don't think you'll be warm enough without a heavy parka, hiking boots with heavy socks, and thermal underwear. Heat escapes from your head and hands, so pack a pair of mittens and a warm cap that covers your ears.

You can also save yourself some worry by bringing a first-aid kit, along with a pair of boots or sturdy sneakers (make sure they're broken in!) for hiking, bicycling, or walking. Binoculars are a must if you want to see our wildlife up close, and a camera will help you remember what you saw here. Once you're tucked away in your room, camper, or tent, it's always nice to have a good book and games to while the night away.

From late spring to fall, there are eight places to stay—six on the South Rim, one on the North Rim, and one in the canyon—with more than 1,000 rooms and cabins total. Accommodations range from basic to deluxe, and the rates vary depending upon the amenities offered. A rustic cabin without bath at the Maswik Lodge costs about $83 a night, while a luxurious suite at the El Tovar Hotel runs over $403 (based on double occupancy; all rates subject to change).

To get the best place for your needs, reserve early through Xanterra reservations (303/297-2757 or 888/297-2757, www.grandcanyonlodges.com). If you're in the park and you want to check on cancellations to make same-night reservations, call Xanterra South Rim (928/638-2631).

If you want to sleep in a tent, recreational vehicle, or under the starry sky, you can choose from five park campgrounds that you can drive to during the months of late May–October. During the winter and early spring, this changes to four campgrounds: Mather, Trailer Village, Desert View, and Tuweep. The Desert View and Tuweep Campgrounds are operated by the NPS on a first-come, first-served basis. Three campgrounds, Mather, North Rim, and Trailer Village, can be reserved in advance. To reserve a site at the Mather or North Rim Campgrounds, contact the National Recreation Reservation Service (877/444-6777, www.recreation.gov).

Sites at Trailer Village are reserved through Xanterra. There are RV sites with 30 and 50 amp electrical service, cable TV, water, sewage, picnic table, and grill at a cost of $28 per site for two people and $2 for each additional person.

You can also bunk down outside the park in various lodges, hotels, motels, private campgrounds, and National Forest campgrounds.

Can Fido and Purr come too?

Sure. You can bring your pets as long as you follow some strict rules. Pets must be kept leashed at all times. They can go with you on paved rim trails and in the rim campgrounds, but those are the only places they can go. They can't follow you on trails below the rims, in buildings, in park buses, or in back-country areas unless they're service/assistance dogs for people with disabilities.

These rules are made for good reason. Our delicate ecosystem isn't ready for the wild mountain Chihuahua or the free-range Labrador. Just about any kind of pet could create problems for the park wildlife and their natural habitats, not to mention other visitors. The rules also protect your pet from possible injury or death from our summertime heat and the narrow trails below the rims. We keep careful watch on these regulations, and we're not shy about handing out citations that can cost you up to $500.

If you bring your pet to the canyon and want to hike below the rims or stay in one of the lodges or hotels where no pets are allowed, the Grand Canyon Village has kennel facilities at Grand Canyon Kennels (off Rowe Well Rd., one mile south of West Rim Drive, 928/638-0534, daily 7:30 A.M.–5 P.M.). Proof of vaccinations is required, and advance reservations are recommended. Call for reservations and more information. Both cats and dogs can be lodged and meals are included. To pick up animals after 5 P.M., you must contact Xanterra Fire and Safety (928/638-2631). There are no kennel facilities on or near the North Rim.

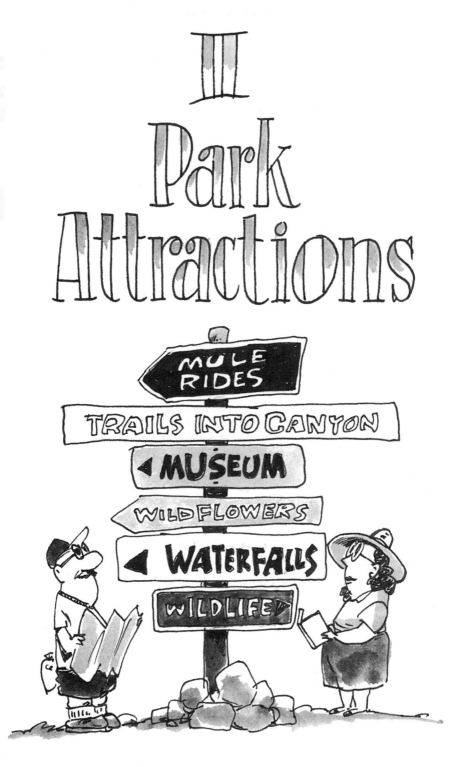

We only have one day to visit; what should we see and do?

Most rangers would tell you it takes several days to sample most of the wonders of the Grand Canyon, but here are a few tips for getting the most out of a single day. For current schedule and activity information, don't forget to check *The Guide* (North or South Rim editions).

South Rim (open year-round)

You can start by getting your bearings at one of the South Rim's two visitor and information centers, the Canyon View Information Plaza and the Desert View Information Station. Here you can orient yourself and learn what activities are planned in the park that day. Next, a visit to the Yavapai Observation Station will provide interesting exhibits about the fossil record in the canyon, as well as an amazing view of the Grand Canyon from large observation windows. Don't miss the history museum and bookstore just off the lobby at the Bright Angel Lodge. You can learn more about the canyon by viewing rotating art exhibits at the Kolb Studio or by going to the Tusayan Museum to see an 800-year-old Native American ruin and exhibit about prehistoric Pueblo life.

You can also join a ranger-led walk or talk about the geology, wildlife, and cultural resources of the Grand Canyon. These free ranger programs are offered daily and change seasonally. Some of the current programs include a sunset talk and short walk that starts from the Yavapai Observation Station an hour before sunset. Nightly in the park, you can join a ranger for an outdoor (June–September) or indoor (October–May)   slide presentation about the ever-changing Grand Canyon. For more information on ranger-led activities, refer to *The Guide*, or the *Getting Around* chapter of this book.

A great way to get the large view of the canyon is to take a free shuttle (year-round) or

On your mark... Get set...

drive (November–April) along Hermit Road (formerly West Rim Drive). You can stop at eight viewing spots during this 16-mile round-trip drive. Or, you can take a private vehicle or commercial bus tour along the scenic 23-mile Desert View Drive (formerly East Rim Drive). You'll see stunning canyon vistas; the Tusayan Indian Ruins; and views of the Painted Desert, Colorado River, San Francisco Peaks, and Vermilion Cliffs from the Watchtower at Desert View. There is no better place to capture the majesty of the Grand Canyon and its surroundings than from the rims. The westernmost and easternmost points will provide the most spectacular views. Be sure to allow enough time (at least two hours for the West Rim and three hours for the East Rim) to linger at each viewpoint along the way.

If you want to slow your touring pace down, I suggest a short walk along one of the rim trails. For those who feel up to the task, a short hike into the canyon along the Bright Angel or South Kaibab Trail will provide awe-inspiring views and a memorable canyon experience. Remember to leave time for lunch at one of the restaurants along the rim before or after you trek into the canyon.

Before you leave home for your trip to the Park, you might want to download a 65-minute audio tour for your mp3 player or iPod (www.tourcaster.com, $12).

North Rim (open May 15–October 15)

Stop at the North Rim Visitor Center, which is located at the south end of the Bright Angel Point parking area. Here you'll find out everything you need to know about what to do and where to go on the North Rim. While at the visitor center, you might want to join one of the daily ranger-led programs that include walks and talks about the history, geology, flora, and fauna of the North Rim.

If you want to see the rim at your own pace, you can try a variety of short- and medium-length rim walks. I would suggest the Bright Angel Point Trail, a half-mile (round-trip) self-guided nature trail that begins at the log shelter at the Grand Canyon Lodge parking area. Or, you can try the three-mile (round-trip) Transept Trail, which follows the rim from the Grand Canyon Lodge to the North Rim Campground and back. For those who are prepared for a longer hike, you can try the 10-mile (round-trip) Uncle Jim Trail, which winds through the rim forest to Uncle Jim's Point overlooking the North Kaibab switchbacks. You can also hike the 10-mile (round-trip) Widforss Trail, which has a self-guided 2.5-mile walk along the rim, then winds through the forest to Widforss Point.

Don't forget to try the dining room at the Grand Canyon Lodge (928/638-2611), which has spectacular views of the canyon. It's open daily during the season, serving breakfast (6:30–10 A.M.), lunch (11:30 A.M.–2:30 P.M.), and dinner (4:45–9:45 P.M.).

For those who want adventure on the back of a mule, you could try the half-day mule trips offered by Canyon Trail Rides (435/679-8665, www.canyonrides.com) that leave daily from the Grand Canyon Lodge. You'll take a bus to the corral at 7:30 A.M. and return by 12:30 P.M. The trip descends 2,400 feet to Supai Tunnel and returns on the same route. The cost is $65, and you must be at least 10 years old.

These are my suggestions. Now it's up to you to design your own way of exploring this magical place. Good luck, and enjoy your day in the Grand Canyon.

You'll probably want to stop first at one of the park visitor centers to get your bearings. Here you can talk with a ranger, view interpretive exhibits, watch a slide presentation, browse the bookstore, and pick up current information about road conditions, hiking trails, and ranger programs in the park's three main geographic areas. Then check out the other information centers listed below to learn more about the Grand Canyon.

SOUTH RIM

Canyon View Information Plaza

This center (928/638-7644, year-round daily 8 A.M.–5 P.M. with additional seasonal hours) is accessible only by free shuttle bus, a one-mile walk or bicycle ride from Market Plaza on the new Greenway Trail, or a short walk from Mather Point. Several outdoor exhibits provide a variety of information about Grand Canyon National Park and what to do once at the park. Outdoor exhibits may be viewed anytime (however the lights at Canyon View Information Plaza are turned off at 9 P.M.). Available facilities include restrooms, pay phones, bookstore, and shuttle bus stops. The canyon rim is only a short stroll away. Check *The Guide* for current schedules and times, or call for more information.

Yavapai Observation Station (Grand Canyon Village)

This facility (Yavapai Point, one mile east of Market Plaza, open year-round) offers panoramic views, artwork, geology exhibits, a large bookstore (daily 8 A.M.–8 P.M.), and ranger-led programs. Call or check *The Guide* for current program schedules and times.

Kolb Studio (Grand Canyon Village)

Located in the Village Historic District, this historic building (Bright Angel Trailhead, year-round daily 8 A.M.–6 P.M. with additional seasonal hours) was built in 1904 as a photography studio. It later housed a soda fountain, a small movie theater, and a gift shop. Today it offers visitors rotating art exhibits, orientation and park information, an auditorium, a bookstore, and ranger-led activities.

Tusayan Museum (Desert View)

A visit to Tusayan Museum (three miles west of Desert View and 22 miles east of Grand Canyon Village on Desert View Dr., year-round, but may be closed due to inclement weather, daily 9 A.M.–5 P.M., free admission) will provide a glimpse of Pueblo Indian life at the Grand Canyon some 800 years ago. For self-guided exploration, a trail leads through the adjacent 800-year-old ruin. Ranger-led ruin tours are offered daily. Educational materials about the park and region are sold in the non-profit bookstore.

Backcountry Office (Maswik Transportation Center)

The Backcountry Office (near Maswik Lodge a few miles west of the visitor center, 928/638-7875, year-round daily 8 A.M.–noon, 1–5 P.M., phone hours Mon.–Fri. 1–5 P.M.) is where you'll find information about camping on the rim, Inner Canyon hiking, and permits for all backcountry camping and hiking.

Desert View Information Station (Desert View)

At Desert View (end of Desert View Drive, 928/638-7893, daily 9 A.M.–5 P.M. except in the winter months when it is open as staffing permits), there's a bookstore operated by the Grand Canyon Association and an NPS information station. Here you can get books, maps, and Park Service publications.

NORTH RIM

North Rim Visitor Center

This facility (south end of the Bright Angel Point parking area, 928/638-7864, mid-May–mid-October daily 8 A.M.–6 P.M.) provides orientation materials, maps, brochures and a bookstore. You can also enjoy seasonal interpretive programs.

Backcountry Office (North Rim Ranger Station)

This office (just north of the main North Rim Campground, 928/638-7875, May 15–October 31 daily 8 A.M.–noon) issues backcountry permits and provides visitors with information on camping and hiking.

Transportation Desks

These desks are located in the lobbies of Maswik, Bright Angel, and Yavapai Lodges, and their operating times vary, depending on season. Information about Phantom Ranch facilities, mule trips, horseback riding, air tours, one-day float trips, and motor coach tours (including wheelchair-accessible vehicles) is available from these desks. Call Xanterra South Rim (928/638-2631, ext. 6015) for more information.

What is the Colorado Plateau?

YOU ARE HERE ↓ x

It's hard to imagine that the Grand Canyon and its plateaus are just a small part of a much larger geologic region called the Colorado Plateau, which encompasses diverse landscapes like deep canyons, towering volcanic mountains, and seven massive plateaus. Elevations in the region range 5,000–12,700 feet above sea level. The Colorado Plateau is bounded by the Mogollon Rim on the south, the Painted Desert and Echo Cliffs on the east, the high plateaus of southern Utah on the north, and the Grand Wash Cliffs on the west. The region comprises five national parks, four national monuments, parts of two national recreation areas, two national forests, two Bureau of Land Management districts, five sovereign Indian nations, numerous wilderness areas, and parts of four states.

The Colorado Plateau is considered a geologic province, a region whose rock formations and landforms share a common history that sets it apart from neighboring regions. Here you'll find one of the most varied assortments of isolated buttes, mesas, odd landforms, and remarkable scenery in the world. Most of the region sits atop thousands of sedimentary rock layers born from ancient seas that advanced and retreated over millions of years. Over long periods of time, these deposits were reshaped through the uplift, tilting, and folding of the earth's crust. Today, the rocks are exposed by the deep canyons that dissect the region and by the sparseness of soil cover and vegetation. That's why the Colorado Plateau provides geologists with an unequaled record of much of the earth's history.

It's also an area where animals, plants, minerals, water, and climate work together in dynamic synchronicity. From a "big picture" point of view, the Colorado Plateau is a very large, interconnected whole that doesn't separate Grand Canyon National Park from the lands that surround it. And, once you take away all the artificially constructed boundaries and put everything together, you have nearly 100 million acres of interactive system that includes a unique landscape, wild animals, and plants that depend upon one another to stay alive—not to mention the million or so human residents who love it. The Colorado Plateau is home to a fascinating mix of cultures, some dating back thousands of years, which are still evident today in the region's Indian nations.

The animals that call this ecosystem home—the desert bighorn sheep, pronghorn antelope, prairie dogs, and others—have adapted over a long period of time to the harsh living conditions and rugged terrain by changing their behavior according to time of day and weather. Animals aren't the only travelers within the region. Plants migrate as well, although they "travel" more slowly as they're carried by animals or weather. The flora and fauna evolved together, surviving cooperatively despite the harshness of the environment.

For the visitor, the Colorado Plateau means more than 130,000 square miles of spectacular scenic and wildland opportunities. It's a place where you can pitch a tent, fish, or boat in one of many rivers and lakes; view some of the country's most beautiful landscapes and wildlife; and enjoy many outdoor activities. Besides the Grand Canyon, the area also offers visitors Zion and Bryce Canyons, Cedar Breaks, Glen Canyon, Rainbow Bridge, the Canyonlands, Capitol Reef, Arches, Four Corners, Mesa Verde, Petrified Forest, the Painted Desert, San Francisco Peaks, and Oak Creek Canyon, among many other natural wonders. As I guide you through this beautiful park, I'll also give you tips on exploring beyond the park, inside the boundaries of the Colorado Plateau.

For more information on the Colorado Plateau area, contact the Grand Canyon Trust (2601 N. Fort Valley Road, Flagstaff, AZ 86001, 928/774-7488 or 888/GCT-5550, fax 928/774-7570, www.grandcanyontrust.org). Their website has a wealth of information about the area, volunteer opportunities, photographs, and programs.

To get you started, here's what's included in the Colorado Plateau area:

National Parks, Monuments, Forests, Recreation Areas
Grand Canyon National Park
Zion National Park
Bryce Canyon National Park
Canyonlands National Park
Arches National Park
Mesa Verde National Park
Sunset Crater National Monument
Wupatki National Monument
Walnut Canyon National Monument
Grand Canyon-Parashant National Monument
Vermilion Cliffs National Monument
Grand Staircase-Escalante National Monument
Lake Mead National Recreation Area
Glen Canyon National Recreation Area
Coconino National Forest
Kaibab National Forest

GREY INDICATES BORDER OF COLORADO PLATEAU

State Parks
Dead Horse Point State Park
Goosenecks State Park
Kodachrome Basin State Park
Goblin Valley State Park

Tribal Lands
Hualapai Reservation
Havasupai Reservation
Navajo Reservation
Hopi Reservation
Kaibab Paiute Reservation

Grand Canyon Facts

- Area: 1.2 million acres or 1,904 square miles
- Length: 277 river miles (Lees Ferry to Grand Wash Cliffs)
- Minimum aerial width: 600 feet at Navajo Bridge (near Lees Ferry)
- Average rim-to-rim aerial width: 10 miles
- Maximum rim-to-rim aerial width: 18 miles
- Average depth: 1 mile
- Total miles of trails in park: 588
- Miles of maintained trails: 51
- Average temperatures (degrees Fahrenheit):

SOUTH RIM	NORTH RIM	INNER CANYON
Low: 18° (January)	Low: 15° (January)	Low: 38° (January)
High: 85° (July)	High: 77° (July)	High: 105° (July)

- Growth in annual visitation:

YEAR	NUMBER OF VISITORS
1919	44,173
1930	166,711
1940	369,234
1950	665,281
1956	1,033,404
(first year to exceed one million visitors)	
1970	2,258,195
1980	2,618,713
1990	3,752,901
1997	4,851,931
1998	4,578,089
1999	4,930,151
2000	4,816,559
2001	4,400,823
2002	4,339,139
2003	4,464,400
2004	4,672,911

- Rim elevations (in feet):

SOUTH RIM	ELEVATION
El Tovar	6,920
Mather Point	7,120
Grandview Point	7,400
Desert View	7,500
Bright Angel Trailhead	6,850
South Kaibab Trailhead	7,200

NORTH RIM	
Grand Canyon Lodge	8,200
Point Imperial	8,800
Cape Royal	7,865
North Kaibab Trailhead	8,240

INNER CANYON	
Indian Garden	3,800
Phantom Ranch	2,400
Roaring Springs	5,000

How was the Grand Canyon formed?

You won't find much agreement on exactly how the canyon was formed. However, geologists who have spent time studying the area seem to agree on many points. Here's the short version of a very long story.

Geologists agree that about two billion years ago, during the Precambrian era, the future Grand Canyon was at the bottom of an ancient and mostly lifeless sea. For tens of millions of years, there had been successive layering of sand, silt, and clay deposits from adjacent continental lands. Volcanic action contributed lava and ash to these deposits. The deposits accumulated over time, and later found themselves buried deep in the earth, where the intense pressure and heat converted the sedimentary rocks to metamorphic rock. The Vishnu schist is an example of this; originally it was a mostly horizontal layered group of sand, shales, mudstones, and volcanics. Metamorphism created a nearly molten mass of twisted and folded material that bore little resemblance to its original state. The cause of all this was a collision about 1.7 billion years ago of two or more continental masses bordering the Grand Canyon region, which probably resulted in construction of a major mountain chain similar to the present-day Rocky Mountains.

As the mountains grew upward and plate collisions waxed and waned, the forces of erosion began their relentless work on the layers of sedimentary deposits in the area that was to become the Grand Canyon. Evidence of this is now shown by the late Precambrian rocks of the Grand Canyon Supergroup. These horizontal rocks were uplifted, tilted, and eroded. Then younger sediments were deposited over these tilted rocks, which were by now deeply buried and changed by heat and pressure to solid rock. Again, uplift brought these rocks to the surface, where the process of erosion could continue its work. Begun in the Paleozoic era, this process of uplift and erosion continued up to some 250 million years ago.

Around 65 million years ago, there was a regional uplift that marked the beginnings of the Rocky Mountains, as well as the Colorado Plateau. This general uplift, which probably continues to the present, resulted in the removal of many thousands of feet of sediment covering the present-day Grand Canyon.

Some six million years ago, volcanic activity broke out in the region, leaving lava flows, spectacular volcanic peaks, and cinder cones that we find throughout the area today. This activity appears to have ended in A.D. 1064.

About one million years ago, there was a massive lava flow in the western Grand Canyon that dammed the canyon for several hundred years, and caused water to back up to around Moab, Utah. The base of this lava flow was only a few dozen feet above the present-day riverbed of the Colorado, indicating that the canyon was close to its present depth. During this same time period, the Grand Canyon was eventually carved by a rising land mass now called the Kaibab uplift.

It's at this point in geologic time that geologists disagree on how the Grand Canyon was actually formed. Although most geologists agree that the canyon was carved by at least two major streams, which eventually joined to form the Colorado River, the stage was now set for the numerous modern theories on the final carving of the Grand Canyon.

One of the most plausible theories has stream systems beginning to flow into the newly formed Gulf of California and quickly eroding westward into the Colorado Plateau, eventually capturing the ancestral Colorado River somewhere west of the Kaibab uplift. This theory suggests that different sections of the Grand Canyon have different ages, formed by two or more river systems.

So there is a long, deep central canyon occupied by the Colorado River. What about the width of the Grand Canyon? Local erosion carved out the side canyons, in all their glory, and the Colorado River acted like a giant conveyor belt to carry the material to the Gulf of California. Through a long process of simple erosion by rainfall, freeze and thaw, gravity, and many other tools, a deep canyon was turned into a Grand Canyon.

What we know is that the forces that created the Grand Canyon worked, sometimes slowly and sometimes in the blink of an eye, over millions of years. Even today, they are at work in the form of rockfalls, landslides, and flash floods that continue to widen the canyon, while the Colorado River strives to lower its bed to sea level. Someday in the future, these agents of erosion, combined with the slowing of downcutting by the Colorado as it nears sea level, could create a broad valley with a slow-moving stream where once there was a grand canyon.

If you're interested in reading the whole story of how the Grand Canyon was formed, get a copy of *A Field Guide to the Grand Canyon* by Stephen R. Whitney, *Grand Canyon Geology* by Stanley Beus and Michael Morales, or *An Introduction to Grand Canyon Geology* by L. Greer Price and Sandra Scott.

Steps in the Creation of the Grand Canyon

1 Pressure within the earth slowly uplifted the surface, causing rivers to run deeper and faster. As the channels deepened, land on both sides was eroded into the river, and the canyon took a V-shape.

2 Erosion worked with many tools, including rain, freeze, and thaw to break down the sides of the main and tributary canyons even further, creating an ever-widening canyon.

3 Over millions of years, the deepening of the river slowed, while the widening continued. In time, the canyon wall may disappear, leaving a flat plain.

Why is there only one Grand Canyon?

If you've ever traveled across the United States or the world, you've probably seen other canyons like the Grand Canyon—just not as big, or with so many wildly different landforms, or with such a range of colors. The name Grand Canyon is fitting in that it's the only one to combine all these elements on such a, well, grand scale. To understand why, you have to look at five main factors that have combined to make this canyon unique in the world.

Geography
You start with a desert climate that has a very powerful river system—in this case, the Colorado and its ancestors—running through it.

Geology
You then add a mile or so of horizontal or nearly horizontal sedimentary rock layers. It is believed that, at one time, thousands of feet of sedimentary rock covered the Grand Canyon region.

Major Geologic Event
Then figure in a major regional uplift allowing the rivers to cut downward through the horizontal rocks. This uplift created the Colorado Plateau, which covers much of the Four Corners region.

Time
You also add just enough time to allow the river system to do its work of eroding the sedimentary rocks, but not so much time that the area has been reduced to sea-level lowlands.

Exposure
Nowhere else in the world is such an authentic geologic record of time visible on such a grand scale as at the Grand Canyon. As you look at the many layers of rocks and the many colors splashed against the canyon walls, and consider the centuries upon centuries it took to form, you begin to understand the enormous feat called the Grand Canyon.

Here's a chart describing
the different layers:

Layer	Estimated Age (Millions of Years)
RIM	
KAIBAB LIMESTONE	250
TOROWEAP	260
COCONINO SANDSTONE	270
HERMIT SHALE	280
SUPAI GROUP	300
SURPRISE CANYON FORMATION	320
REDWALL LIMESTONE	330
TEMPLE BUTTE	370
UNDIVIDED DOLOMITE	500
MUAV LIMESTONE	530
BRIGHT ANGEL SHALE	540
TAPEATS SANDSTONE	550
GRAND CANYON SUPER GROUP	800 MILLION TO 1.2 BILLION YEARS
VISHNU SCHIST	

33

What's so special about canyon nights?

Far away from the glare of big city lights and pollution, the recurring drama of the night sky over the Grand Canyon is hard to describe. During the full moon, the canyon comes alive with looming shadows that transform the Inner Canyon. The new moon lifts the veil of the Milky Way and reveals the glow of infinite stars emblazoned across a black universe. On moonless nights, the canyon is dark beyond compare. With no streetlights, you're lucky to see your hand in front of your face, much less a trail or a sidewalk. Remember, a flashlight will be your best friend on these nights.

Here are some suggestions for experiencing canyon nights:

South Rim

This is where you'll find the most popular and crowded spots for experiencing canyon nights. Because it's so dark, the safest spots include the open areas around the hotels along the rim (although exterior lighting may spoil the impact). More adventuresome night watchers can try Mather, Yavapai, Pima, and Hopi Points. Walking the trail from El Tovar to Yavapai Point at night is an entirely different experience than it is during the day. Dress warmly, stay on the trail, carry a flashlight—and don't forget to stop and look up every so often.

North Rim

Because of its orientation, dense tree cover, and fewer established trails, the North Rim offers fewer opportunities for viewing canyon nights than the South Rim. The exceptions are the open areas around the Grand Canyon Lodge; the veranda at the Lodge offers great views. One of the North Rim's finest experiences is the walk to Bright Angel Point on a moonlit night. The shadowed canyon becomes otherworldly, and you can see the far-off twinkling lights of the South Rim Village.

Definitely along the rim. Although most visitors would say there's no one "best" spot to see the sun rise and fall over the canyon, I can tell you some of the most popular spots, as well as some of my favorites.

South Rim

This is where you'll find the most popular—and crowded—spots for viewing a spectacular sunrise over the canyon. Some of the most popular spots include open areas around the hotels along the rim and Yaki, Yavapai, Mather, and Hopi Points. The most crowded of the overlooks on any given summer day is Mather Point. For outstanding sunset views, you can try around the hotels or Yavapai, Hopi, and Pima Points. My choice for experiencing an unparalleled sunrise is Mather Point and Lipan Point for a spectacular sunset. You can find your own "favorite spot" by picking almost any point along the South Rim that has sweeping views to the east and west.

North Rim

Because of its orientation and fewer number of established trails, the North Rim offers more limited opportunities for viewing sunrise and sunset. The exceptions are the open areas around the Grand Canyon Lodge (even the veranda at the Lodge offers great views), Bright Angel Point, the Cape Royal picnic area, and Point Imperial, where you'll be treated to a great sunrise.

Wherever you go, don't forget to arrive early at your viewing spot. Sunrise and sunset times are available online (www.nps.gov/grca/planyourvisit/sunrise_set_moon.htm) and in *The Guide.* Now, let's go sun hunting!

Where can we
see Waterfalls?

Although there are numerous waterfalls in Grand Canyon National Park, most require so much effort and time to get to that you'll need 3–7 days to see them. The exception is the Roaring Springs waterfall and picnic area, which can be accessed by hiking 4.7 miles down the North Kaibab Trail from the North Rim. For more information about this trail, call the North Rim Visitor Center (928/638-7864, May 15–October 15).

The waterfalls that are the easiest to reach from the South Rim are located in the canyon, but outside park boundaries. This spectacular series of four, blue-green waterfalls can be found on the Havasupai Indian Reservation in the western Grand Canyon, near the village of Supai. This is one of the most beautiful and remote areas of the canyon and is accessible only by foot, on horseback, or by limited helicopter service.

The trail to the village of Supai begins at Hualapai Hilltop, which is 66 miles from Peach Springs, Arizona. Peach Springs is on old Highway 66, north of Interstate 40. Driving time from Grand Canyon Village on the South Rim to Hualapai Hilltop is approximately 4–5 hours. In the village of Supai is the Havasupai Lodge, with year-round overnight accommodations and 24 rooms, all nonsmoking. A cafe in the village serves breakfast, lunch, and dinner accepting cash, credit cards, and debit cards. Special permits to visit the reservation and village of Supai are required, and cost $35 per adult, $17.50 for kids 12 and under. You can obtain a permit by contacting the Havasupai Tourist Enterprise (camping reservations 928/448-2121, 928/448-2141, 928/448-2174, or 928/448-2180, lodging reservations 928/448-2111 or 928/448-2201, www. havasupaitribe.com).

Getting to the village of Supai by foot from Hualapai Hilltop means an 8-mile walk down a large tributary canyon on the south side of the Colorado River. While the hike down to the village is easy to moderate, be sure you take plenty of water and rest often, especially in hot weather. The trip by saddle and packhorses is less strenuous—except for the horses and mules—and takes 3–4 hours. Cost is $150 from Hilltop to the campground and back; $75 one-way from or to the campground; $120 round-trip from Hilltop to the Lodge; and $70 one-way from Hilltop to Lodge. If you're planning to travel on foot or by saddle and packhorses, allow at least three days for the trip. That way, you'll be able to spend one entire day exploring and enjoying the falls.

Helicopter service to the village of Supai is available in the summer

(March 15–October 15) Sunday, Monday, Thursday, and Friday approximately 10 A.M.–1 P.M. In winter (October 16–March 14), they run on Sunday and Friday approximately 10 A.M.– 1 P.M. at a cost of $85 per person. For more information, contact Airwest Helicopters of Arizona (928/516-2790).

From the village, the falls are a short, easy walk down Havasu Canyon. Distances from the village to the falls are: Navajo Falls 1.5 miles, Havasu Falls and campground 2 miles, Mooney Falls 3 miles, and Beaver Falls 5 miles. From Beaver Falls, the trail continues another 4 miles until it reaches the Colorado River. There are many places along the trail to picnic, so plan for an entire day to enjoy one of the most beautiful walks you'll ever take.

· Havasu Falls ·

What kinds of animals live in the park?

Since the Grand Canyon ranges from 1,200 feet at the canyon's western floor to 9,200 feet on the North Rim, it is home to a unique variety of animals that are indigenous to both desert and mountain environments. These extreme elevation changes in a relatively small area support a wide range of habitats, from aquatic to desert scrub to coniferous forest, that would normally be found only by traveling from Mexico to Canada. Now, let's take a look at the inhabitants.

Of the 373 species of birds that have been observed at the Grand Canyon, 168 nest in the area and many live there year-round, including the double-crested cormorant, great blue heron, mallard duck, red-tailed hawk, Peregrine falcon, Gambel's quail, mourning dove, great horned owl, and canyon wren.

There are 17 fish species, including 5 native species that still live in the Grand Canyon stretch of the Colorado River. Their numbers have decreased due to damming, but there is a small remnant population at the junction of the Colorado and Little Colorado Rivers. They include the humpback chub, flannelmouth sucker, bluehead sucker, razorback sucker, and speckled dace. The park also has nine types of frogs, toads, and salamanders who are year-round residents, including the Utah tiger salamander, Rocky Mountain toad, and canyon tree frog. Hikers will rarely see any of our 47 kinds of reptiles, including the northern plateau lizard, mountain short-horned lizard, Sonoran gopher snake, California king snake, and the very-seldom-seen pinkish Grand Canyon rattlesnake, which is found only in the Inner Canyon.

Of our 91 different types of mammals, 11 species are found only on the North Rim, and 9 only on the South Rim. The most famous of these are two species of tassel-eared squirrels, which are quite similar except for the coloration on their undersides and tails. The Kaibab squirrel of the North Rim is found nowhere else in the world. The Abert squirrel of the South Rim has been seen as far north as Colorado and as far south as Mexico. It seems as though the little Abert squirrel must have crossed over to the North Rim at one point when pine trees were more plentiful. Later, as the climate became more arid and the pines retreated to higher elevations, the squirrels on the North Rim were isolated from their kin and slowly evolved into a different species.

Of the more abundant mammals, here are some that you might expect to see when you visit the Grand Canyon. On the rims, look for the rock pocket mouse, nocturnal ringtail cat (which looks like a wide-eyed raccoon), western spotted skunk (look for them between the Bright Angel Lodge and El Tovar Hotel during the summer), wild turkey, mule deer, elk, and coyote. In the Inner Canyon, you might see the desert bighorn on the Bright Angel and Kaibab Trails just below the South Rim, California bat, white-tailed antelope, canyon mouse, and desert wood rat. With the exception of squirrels, many of the smaller animals are hard to find because they escape the daytime heat in burrows, caves, rock crevices, tree cavities, and other shady areas. Many of them are partly nocturnal, coming out during the cool night for food. As a result, the predatory animals are also nocturnal. Canyon animals have adapted very well to the harsh environment by beating the heat.

Water is the primary necessity for the survival of Grand Canyon animals, and they have developed clever ways of getting it. Smaller animals that don't have the ability to search widely for water, including squirrels, mice, and kangaroo rats, are able to get enough water from the food they eat or as part of the normal process of digesting their food. An interesting example of adaptation to the desert environment is the antelope ground squirrel, which supplements its primarily vegetarian diet with insects, thereby increasing its moisture supply. You might say that the Grand Canyon has bred a bunch of smart, year-round inhabitants.

What are the best ways to spot wildlife?

Looking for animals in the hot, arid climate of the Grand Canyon can be a challenging task, since many animals use hiding places to escape the heat. It requires time, patience, and cunning observation.

The first thing to know about our desert residents is that they feed in the early morning and early evening hours. To better your chances of seeing wildlife, try walking the rim in the morning when there's still a chill in the air, or take a walk just before or after sunset. These are also the best times to lose the crowds, which tend to frighten away our quiet desert animals. Wear fabrics that blend naturally with the desert colors. If you're walking, move slowly, and if you see an animal, avoid sudden movements. Don't forget binoculars for an up-close view. Most importantly, don't try to get too close to the animals.

Here are some hints about places to view certain animals. Year-round, look for the tassel-eared Abert squirrel feeding on the tender shoots and pinecones of the tall ponderosa pines throughout the South Rim. The Kaibab squirrel, a close relative of the Abert, thrives in the ponderosa pine forests of the North Rim. In the developed areas along the rims, you'll probably run into rock squirrels begging for food handouts from visitors. If you're hiking, keep an eye out for our more elusive predator, the bobcat, who frequents the North and South Rims. A more common sight is the coyote, hunting throughout the park from rim to river. The most commonly seen mammal on the South Rim is the mule deer, who travels in and out of the canyon with great speed and agility.

One of the largest hoofed mammals in the park, the desert bighorn, prefers the rocky slopes of the Inner Canyon to the rim. Like other mammals of the desert, they are most likely to be seen near sources of water like springs, seeps, or pools of summer rain.

The handsome, nonpoisonous gopher snake is the only snake you're likely to see along the rim. If you're walking in open rocky

Wake up, honey, Time to go see the deer feeding

NNNNH

40

areas near the rim, you might also catch a glimpse of the southern plateau lizard, with a blue patch on either side of its throat.

The birds you'll see most frequently are the mountain chickadee, with its black bib and white stripe over its eye, and the nuthatch, deftly flying through the coniferous forests along the rims in search of insects. Look to the sky if you're standing on the rim during the summer months, and you might glimpse a white-throated swift or violet-green swallow slashing through the air in pursuit of insects. Or, you might hear the distinctive caw of the black raven flying in the canyon or perched along the rim.

But remember, when you feed wild animals, you're not doing them a favor. In fact, many of the animals that have become accustomed to human food at the Grand Canyon end up starving to death because they have ingested foods that they can't process. Please help keep our animals wild and healthy by not feeding them. **Please remember that it is illegal to approach or feed wildlife in Grand Canyon National Park.**

Bighorns and Burros in the Grand Canyon

Between the late 1860s and early 1900s, miners and prospectors arrived in the Grand Canyon in search of the copper, silver, lead, zinc, uranium, and asbestos that had been discovered in the area. To get heavy equipment and supplies in and out of the canyon, miners used sturdy burros as pack animals. As mining activity in the area ended, mining claims were abandoned and burros were left behind, and eventually became a feral population of thousands.

The burros' progeny created an ecological nightmare in the latter part of the 1900s, when an ever-increasing burro population began competing for the same resources used by the bighorn sheep and other indigenous animals. Burro Canyon in the park is so named because of the thousands of burros that used to flock to the site for water.

As the wild burros flourished, the population of bighorn sheep decreased dramatically. In the late 1970s to early 1980s, most of the burros were captured and removed from the Grand Canyon through the efforts of the National Park Service and private humane societies. Removal activities peaked in 1980–1981, with a major effort by the Fund for Animals to round up all remaining 500 burros.

Today, bighorn sheep in the park have again become a stable and healthy population, and burros can still be found in several remote canyons of the Hualapai and Havasupai Indian Reservations.

Sorry, no petting zoo privileges here. Every time someone feeds an animal at the Grand Canyon, a little bit of the "wild" is stolen from our wildlife. Human food can not only damage the animals' health, but also endanger their survival by luring them away from their natural habitats.

Feeding one of our cute chipmunks or squirrels and capturing the moment on film might seem like a good idea, but their teeth are sharp and there's always the possibility of infection. In the case of a wild animal bite, doctors usually recommend a series of painful rabies shots. Not a fun way to spend your vacation.

Federal law prohibits people from feeding or approaching our wildlife, and for good reason. Our animals may look harmless, but most are capable of causing injury, and in extreme cases even death, to people who get too close. If an animal reacts to your presence, you're probably too close.

Besides, you can learn more about animal habits through quiet observation than interaction. For good photographs of animals, take a look at the huge selection of books and postcards in the stores throughout the park.

Yep, you guessed it: chipmunks and squirrels. Okay, maybe it wasn't your first guess. Nevertheless, the same cute little critters you try to feed and photograph on the rock walls between Verkamp's and the Bright Angel Lodge have the distinction of being the Grand Canyon's most notorious biters. They're especially ornery when people try to lure them by pretending to have food, just to get a good picture. Year-round, the most dangerous animal in the Grand Canyon is the one you try to feed.

You also can run into these little critters on the trail. If you set your pack down on a heavily traveled trail such as Bright Angel, it's an open invitation to ground squirrels. They can rip a hole in an expensive pack in the time it takes to take a sip of water.

In the canyon, scorpions are common, and stings often occur. The good news is that while scorpion stings are painful, they rarely cause serious health problems. If stung, apply cold compresses for pain relief and monitor any symptoms. The bad news is that scorpions are small and hard to see due to their light tan color. If you're camping or backpacking, shake out boots, clothing, and bedding before getting into them.

Although the reclusive bobcat and rarely seen mountain lion naturally avoid contact with humans, they are wild animals, and caution should always be used when you're in their habitat. Keep an eye on your kids, who may think it's fun to run out of your sight and unknowingly into the path of a wild animal. Even mule deer can be dangerous if surprised. The other animals to watch out for are the coyote, who appears to be unafraid of people; the raven, who is not shy about taking food right out of people's backpacks; and the occasional black bear on the North Rim.

Most injuries at the canyon result from people getting too close to animals. The moral is, don't be fooled into thinking the cute little ones are harmless. Fleas carried by ground squirrels have been known to spread disease. And remember, any animal that begs for food is potentially dangerous. Let's just say it's best if people and animals at the canyon maintain a long-distance relationship. And remember, approaching, feeding, hunting, or removing wildlife from the park is against the law.

The most important thing to know is that even though they're around, you probably won't see many snakes and lizards at the Grand Canyon. Also, they are rarely found above 7,000 feet. Although they are well suited for life in the desert, most reptiles escape the heat by burrowing underground or hiding in shaded rock crevices, coming out to forage during the cooler morning and early evening hours. Several canyon species are nocturnal. Most of the snakes in the canyon, with the exception of several species of rattlesnake, are harmless to humans.

Most Grand Canyon reptiles hibernate to avoid the winter cold. That's why you'll almost never see snakes on the higher plateaus, where temperatures are coldest. Reptiles are most abundant in the lower, warmer zones of the Inner Canyon. If you're walking in the canyon in the early morning, you might see snakes and lizards warming themselves on rocks or on open ground exposed to the sun. A chuckwalla will bask in the sun on ledges, and, if threatened, will slip into a crack in the rock and puff up, making it extremely difficult to dislodge him. At dusk, you might spot reptiles in places that have retained the day's heat, like stones or pavement.

Reptiles at the canyon come in a wide variety of lizards and snakes. There are even three subspecies of rattlesnake that are found only at the Grand Canyon. These include the rarely seen Grand Canyon rattlesnake, with its pinkish color and diamond-shaped pattern on its skin. It's found in the Inner Canyon and has a distinctive

REPTILES

44

rattle. The Hopi rattlesnake, which lives in the Inner Canyon and along the South Rim, is pinkish, greenish, or grayish in color, with well-defined splotches. The Great Basin rattlesnake is found in the Inner Canyon or along the North Rim. Color varies from light brown to gray, with dark, well-defined, narrow splotches.

Although you may never see one, reptiles—both harmless and venomous—are a natural part of the landscape of the Grand Canyon.

Chuckwalla

Any great birding spots?

Although the Grand Canyon is more famous for rocks than birds, it still has more than its share of feathered residents. Throughout the year, 373 species of birds call the canyon home (with 168 known species that nest here), including about 21 kinds of hawks, eagles, and falcons. The birds range in size from the tiny Rufous hummingbird and Bell's Vireo to the great blue heron and California condor.

For avid birders, there is a vast array of interesting birds and habitats to choose from in and around the Grand Canyon, including many species that live here year-round. While some of our desert species depend upon open water for moisture, many birds get enough from the insects they eat. The best way to see the greatest number of birds at the Grand Canyon is to visit a variety of habitats—and that means hiking. A day hike to Indian Garden or an overnight hike to Phantom Ranch offers a wonderful variety of birds. Here are some other areas you might want to check out.

Let's start with aquatic habitats with standing water along the rims. This includes the sewage lagoons (artificial ponds that have become popular resting spots for migrating birds and provide some great birding opportunities) and cattle tanks on the South Rim and lakes on the North Rim (May–November). In the summer, you'll probably see the violet-green swallow and the spotted sandpiper at the ponds and tanks as well as all over both rims. If you're lucky, you might also catch a glimpse of a migrating double-crested cormorant, great blue heron, or mallard duck around the ponds.

Along both rims in the pinyon pine and ponderosa pine forests mixed with firs, aspens, spruce, and oaks above 7,000 feet, some of the most commonly seen birds include the red-tailed hawk, American kestrel, mourning dove (summers), great horned owl, common raven, rock and canyon wren, western bluebird, and American robin. Other commonly seen birds along the rims include the mountain chickadee, white-breasted nuthatch, dark-eyed junco, and juniper titmouse, as well as the Steller's and western scrub jay. If you're here in the summer, you might catch a glimpse of the house finch, brown-headed cowbird, black-chinned hummingbird, and turkey vulture. Throughout September and October, keep a special watch out for the numerous species of raptors that migrate through the area. During the winter months, look for the white-crowned sparrow. All along the South Rim is prime bird-watching territory, especially along the abyss on the West Rim where you might see peregrine falcons flying high overhead. On the North Rim, you can also expect to see wild turkey, Clark's nutcracker, and perhaps Williamson's sapsucker.

As you go down the canyon, you're likely to see many of the same species in habitats ranging from the grasslands of the Toroweap Valley and meadows of the Kaibab Plateau (4,600 feet) to Mojave and Sonoran desert scrub (below 2,000 feet).

At the lower elevations of the canyon, you'll find aquatic habitats with flowing water including the Colorado River and its tributaries, such as Bright Angel and Garden Creeks. In the summer, look for the blue-winged teal and spotted sandpiper, common sights on the river. During the winter months, look for the bald eagle along the banks of the river and its tributaries. Riparian woodland habitats along the banks of the Colorado River and its tributaries are home to feathered residents like the Lucy's warbler, Bell's vireo, willow fly-catcher, hooded oriole, and blue grosbeak.

That should get you started. Don't forget to take along a pair of binoculars for viewing our feathered residents. If you want to read more about birds in the Grand Canyon, I recommend *A Field Guide to the Grand Canyon* by Stephen Whitney.

Condors in the Canyon

If you are lucky during your visit to the Grand Canyon, you might catch a glimpse of a rare and majestic bird, the California condor. The largest land bird in North America with nearly 9.5-foot wingspans and weighing up to 22 pounds, condors were more common in this area in the past; but shootings, poisonings, and collisions with power lines drastically reduced their numbers.

In 1996, six condors were released in the Vermilion Cliffs just west of Lees Ferry. Currently about 60 condors ply the skies over Arizona and many frequent the canyon environment. In the summer of 2003, the first condor chick fledged in Arizona in more than a century. All of them have been reintroduced from other locations, thanks to the combined efforts of the Peregrine Fund, the U.S. Fish and Wildlife Service, the Arizona Game and Fish Department, the National Park Service, and the U.S. Bureau of Land Management.

All of the condors in the Grand Canyon area carry wing tags to allow research staff to track and identify particular birds. Another identifying factor is that condors have no feathers on their heads. Young condors have a grayish-black head color, while adult condors have an orange head color.

Young condors are curious birds and may be attracted to human environments such as campsites, so avoid damage to your belongings by not leaving equipment unattended. If you are lucky enough to encounter a condor, do not approach or attempt to feed the bird. Please report anyone seen harassing or harming a condor to park management.

For additional information about the California condor relocation project, please contact the Peregrine Fund (208/362-3716, www.peregrine fund.org) or the Arizona Game and Fish Department (California Condor Project Coordinator, 928/214-1249, www.azgfd.gov/w_c/ california_condor.shtml). The Peregrine Fund website is an excellent source of up-to-date information. (They even give bios for each bird.)

J ust as the canyon supports a diversity of animal life, so too does it host an array of plants. At every elevation you will see plant life adapted to the various life zones represented in the canyon. Let's take a look at the major categories of plants that are found in the Grand Canyon and find out where they grow.

Ferns and Related Plants

The ferns and allied plants like horsetails and spike moss are among the oldest in the fossil record. Of the earth's 10,000 types of ferns and related plants,

about 20 are found in the Grand Canyon. Because of the steep terrain, many canyon ferns are adapted to growing in cliff crevices, where enough soil and moisture are found. A few grow in moist places like seeps, springs, and stream banks, while others prefer more arid habitats like the canyon's limestone cliffs. Near streams, ponds, springs, and especially the Colorado River, you'll see horsetails and scouring rushes. Look for the maidenhair fern near seeps and springs below the rims and brittle fern in the nearby rocky areas. In moist crevices throughout the canyon walls, look for Eaton's lip ferns. In the more arid habitats, like the dry rocky slopes and cliffs below the rim, you'll find the slender lip and the lip fern, the most abundant dry-habitat fern in the park. In the limestone rocks

Male Fern

below the rim, keep an eye out for the wavy cloak fern. In the North Rim forests, you'll find western bracken.

Flowering Plants

With its varied topography and climate, the Grand Canyon supports over 1,500 species of flowering plants, including annuals, perennials, wildflowers, cacti, and trees and shrubs. These are normal plants that

Golden Columbine

have adapted themselves to the dry, blistering temperatures of the Inner Gorge and the snowy, freezing winters of the Kaibab Plateau. In a word, they're tough! Plants that live in the scorching areas of the Inner Canyon grow far apart from each other to minimize competition for water. Most desert wildflowers adapt to the climate by blooming only in the early spring, when soils are moist and temperatures mild. If rainfall is below normal, they may even remain dormant for several years. Most of the plants that grow in the Inner Canyon have adapted to heat and drought by modifying their leaves and stems. That's why you'll see many canyon plants that have small, coated leaves, hair and thorns, special root systems, and succulents that store moisture in leaves and stems.

Desert Tobacco

On the high plateaus where temperatures dip below freezing even on summer nights, the plants become dormant during the winter (with the first snows of autumn) and put out rapid shoots at the first hint of summer (shortly after the snowpack melts).

Here are some of the flowering plants that are commonly seen along the South and North Rims: prickle poppy, sego lily, rock mat, bristly hiddenflower, Wheeler's thistle, Rocky Mountain pussytoe, sulfur flower, bladderpod, stickleaf, broom snakeweed, skyrocket, carmine thistle, perennial rock cress, wire lettuce, hill lupine, toadflax penstemon, green gentian, deers ears, specklepod, and tidy fleabane. Below the rims look for the Grand Canyon phacelia, Mohave aster, twining snapdragon, Goodding verbena, climbing milkweed, purple bladderpod, trailing four o'clock, firecracker penstemon, Utah beardtongue, crimson monkeyflower, greenstem paperflower, spiny goldenweed, parry tackstem, groundcherry, desert trumpet, desert tobacco, sacred datura, sand verbena, and watercress.

Cacti

There are about 24 species of cacti found in the Grand Canyon. Noted for their amazing flowers, the blossoms of canyon cacti are mostly red or reddish-purple, and sometimes yellow. Grand Canyon cacti also tend to be shrubby, typically forming low mats or clumps. Most of the varieties of cacti are found in the canyon, where they grow in hot, arid places among rocks, grasses, and shrubs. Some examples you might encounter are cottontop cactus, Engelmann hedgehog cactus,

Sego Lily

California barrel cactus, fishhook cactus, beavertail cactus, and pancake pear cactus. On the rims, keep an eye out for the desert prickly pear and the grizzly bear cactus.

Hedgehog Cactus

Trees and Shrubs

The Grand Canyon is home to about 200 species of trees and shrubs. Although naturally insulated from temperature extremes by bark and woody branches, they still adapt to the cold by lowering the water content of their sap. The remaining sap acts like antifreeze, freezing at lower temperatures than water. The limbs of the trees and shrubs are also flexible, so they won't break under the weight of snow. You'll probably notice some bent trees on the steep canyon slopes. This is the result of the downward movement of the snowpack, which causes young trees to bend just above the base.

Along the South and North Rims, the more common trees you'll find include the ponderosa pine, Colorado pinyon, Utah juniper, and Gambel oak. On the North Rim, which has higher elevations and a cooler, wetter environment, you'll also see white fir, subalpine fir, Engelmann spruce, Douglas fir, common juniper, bigtooth maple, and quaking aspen. Some of the shrubs you may run into along both rims include the arroyo willow, Mormon tea, banana yucca, century plant, wax currant, cliff rose, Apache plume, littleleaf and true mountain mahogany, rabbitbrush, Utah serviceberry, shrubby creambush, big sagebrush, and the mock orange. Along the North Rim you'll also find the greenleaf manzanita, water birch, chokecherry, creeping barberry, and the New Mexican locust.

Yellow Ragweed

Below the rims, some of the trees and shrubs found primarily in the canyons include the salt-cedar or tamarisk, canyon grape, western redbud, greasebush, brittlebush, trixis, arrowweed, Fremont cottonwood, red willow, seep-willow, blackbrush, yellowleaf silktassel, catclaw acacia, honey mesquite, creosote bush, and ocotillo.

For further reading on the plants of the Grand Canyon, be sure to pick up a copy of *A Field Guide to the Grand Canyon* by Stephen Whitney.

Where are the best places to see wildflowers?

Our hot summers and freezing winters limit the park's growing season, but throughout the Grand Canyon you will find a short but spectacular display of wildflowers at every elevation and in all types of habitats.

Generally, wildflowers in the park grow only in mild temperatures and in soil that is moist. Their growth depends entirely on the winter season; a late, wet winter means more wildflowers. A dry winter does not bode well for you flower hunters. Following germination in early spring, the development of roots and shoots is fast, with flowers and seeds produced in a few weeks, after which the plants die.

South Rim

When the warm temperatures arrive on the South Rim you'll see wildflowers in profusion along the roads and in the forests. Around the visitor center look for colorful patches of lupine, and, depending on the winter rains, the twice-blooming cliff rose. Because of the relatively mild temperatures on the higher-elevation rim, wildflowers can be seen here from spring (when they're most plentiful) through fall. Some of the more commonly seen wildflowers include baby white asters, yellow sunflowers, golden western wallflowers, orange globemallow, and rabbitbrush. In the woodland forests of the rim, look for the orange-red Indian paintbrush, the purple hill lupine, and, occasionally, a prickly pear cactus.

Cliff Rose

North Rim

Spring on the North Rim is the best time to see an amazing array of shapes and colors. Some of the most impressive displays can be found along the road to Cape Royal and Point Imperial and in the meadows along the rim, especially those at the trailheads for the Uncle Jim and Widforss Trails. Just below the rim, in moist shady places, look for the wild strawberry and the bright red skyrocket. In sunny areas, watch for the white flowers of yarrow and the long yellow flowers of the Utah deervetch. In the meadows you'll probably see the orange mountain dandelion and the yellow flowers of the pale mountain dandelion.

Inner Canyon

Below the rims in the Grand Canyon, you'll find a mosaic of wildflowers March–June, with some wildflowers blooming into October following the summer monsoon thunderstorms. Some of the wildflowers to look for include the blue to purple flowers of the Grand Canyon phacelia in the Inner Gorge area of the western Grand Canyon; the white or blue flowers of the Mohave aster on the talus slopes and dry places on the canyon walls; the bright red flowers of the crimson monkeyflower in shady seeps and stream banks in the canyon; the magenta flowers of the trailing four o'clock in the canyon, Inner Gorge, and Tonto Platform; and the purple lobes of the twining snapdragon vine, found on shaded ledges in the Inner Gorge and the side canyons.

Prickle Poppy

You'll also see flowering cacti, mostly on the canyon floor March–October.

Here are some hints on what to look for as you travel around the park:

- Evening primroses, on both rims, along roads, and in open areas. From May until summer, these flowers open in the evening and close in the morning sun.

- The stately sego lily, the state flower of Utah, in open areas on both rims.

- The Utah agave, a widespread flowering plant found at every elevation from rim to river.

- Cliff rose along open areas on the South Rim and along Bright Angel and Kaibab Trails. The white flowers are common April–June.

- Desert phlox, along the same trails, in April. The flowers vary from white to deep pink.

- Prickle poppy, which grows in many disturbed areas and begins to flower after many of the other spring flowers have gone to seed.

For more information, refer to the books listed in the *Further Reading* chapter, including of Art Phillips's *Grand Canyon Wildflowers.*

To tell you the truth, the Grand Canyon wouldn't be my first choice for fall color. We do have golden displays of cottonwoods along tributary streams throughout the canyon, oaks scattered along the rims and in the side canyons, and aspens bordering meadows on the North Rim and in the higher elevations, but they're scattered in small pockets.

In the nearby areas, the best place to see fall color is outside park boundaries, along 50 miles of Highway 180, between Flagstaff and the Highway 64 junction. You can also see glorious color around the San Francisco Peaks. From late August through October, cottonwood, willow, and aspens ignite the area with gold. But watch out: By early November you could get hit by the first winter storms and road closures.

As you leave the Grand Canyon via the South Entrance Road, follow Highway 64 for 28 miles until you reach the Highway 180 turnoff. This curvy, two-lane road with lots of hills winds through Kaibab National Forest. You'll see areas of sagebrush opening to ponderosa and pinyon-juniper-aspen forests, followed by a large stand of aspen that frames the San Francisco Peaks just outside of Flagstaff. This is a distinctly volcanic landscape that gives rise to the majestic San Francisco Peaks: Humphreys Peak (12,643 ft., the highest point in Arizona), Kendrick Peak (10,418 ft.), Agassiz Peak (12,356 ft.), and Doyle Peak (11,969 ft.).

As you drive toward Flagstaff on Highway 180, take some time to stop and look around at the awesome landscape. There are several turnouts that provide overviews of this area and its mountains. Just pay attention to traffic, which reaches its height during the summer months. Don't forget to pick up a good road map of the South and North Kaibab National Forest, for sale at the visitor center.

Here are some other suggestions for good fall color viewing:

- For spectacular views of the Kaibab Forest, visit the Snowbowl ski area at the San Francisco Peaks, and take the chair lift.

- Drive along the network of forest service dirt roads that circle and traverse the San Francisco Peaks area (not recommended during wet weather).

What Indian tribe built the Desert View Watchtower?

Although it looks like it could have been built by one of the area's Native American tribes, the Watchtower was actually designed in the early 1930s by Mary Colter, architect for the Fred Harvey Company and Santa Fe Railway. She designed it as a gift shop and resting place offering dramatic views of the canyon for the company's sightseeing tours.

Colter spent months traveling around the Southwest, studying and sketching remains of prehistoric Pueblo towers in the Four Corners. This enabled her to capture the texture and spirit of ancient Native American buildings. Colter also spent time studying the Desert View site to take advantage of every detail of the panoramic view and to design a structure that fit with the surrounding landforms and landscape.

Once she determined the precise location for the building, she had the Santa Fe Railway build a 70-foot-high metal and wood scaffolding. It became the highest point on the South Rim, with 360-degree views of the Painted Desert, San Francisco Peaks, Vermilion Cliffs, and beyond.

Stones for the exterior were gathered from the local area, and interior furnishings were handcrafted from tree trunks and wood burls of local species. Colter hired local Hopi artist Fred Kabotie to paint a tribal mural in the ceremonial room, or kiva. In the center of the room is a beautiful sand painting of a Hopi Indian Snake altar.

Since the building opened in 1933, the Watchtower at Desert View has been a favorite place for both visitors and locals to capture the spectacular vistas of the canyon. On May 28, 1987, the building was designated as a United States National Historic Landmark.

For more information on Mary Colter, refer to the *Quick Reference* chapter or pick up a copy of *Mary Colter: Builder Upon the Red Earth* by Virginia Grattan.

Mary Colter
Photo courtesy Grand Canyon National Park Museum Collection, #16950

What was life like for the Canyon's native people?

Although we don't know very much about their lives, we know that humans have been a part of the Grand Canyon region for at least 4,000 years. A major clue comes in the form of hundreds of mysterious stick figures found in limestone caves high on the canyon walls. Because the stick figures resemble animals, including some stuck with a small spear and placed in shrine-like formations, most archaeologists think they were good luck totems for hunters.

Where did these people come from? If we go back in time about 12,000 years, we learn that people crossed Russia's Siberian peninsula to Alaska in North America during the Ice Age. Many of these ancient people ventured southward into the United States, Mexico, and South America.

Artifact dating tells us that people probably lived in or around the Grand Canyon for at least part of the year, leaving the stick figures made from twigs of willow and cottonwood in the caves and giving us a vital link to the past.

About 1,500 years ago, the ancestral Pueblo people, sometimes known as the Anasazi (ancient ones), arrived in the region now known as the Colorado Plateau and began living in and around the Grand Canyon. These people excelled in handicrafts, perfecting basketry and the manufacture of other functional items like sandals, bags, and clothing. For cold weather, they interlaced rabbit fur or deerskin strips to make capes and blankets. They also made beautiful ceramic bowls, ladles, jars, pitchers, and even canteens.

Split-twig figurine from willow. 4,000 years old. Similar to others found in Canyon caves.

For a constant source of meat, the ancestral Pueblo people tamed and kept wild turkeys. They also hunted deer, antelope, and bighorn sheep, and gathered pinyon nuts, yucca pods, and cactus fruits. Their skills in the field resulted in small, controlled crops of corn, beans, and squash. They even developed irrigation systems using water collected from rains on the Colorado Plateau.

Skilled and prolific builders, the ancestral Pueblo people constructed cliff dwellings of mud and stone. Later, more intricate structures were sometimes built several stories high, called pueblos (from the Spanish word meaning "village"). Without the help of horses, which would arrive in the 15th century, they built pueblos in areas that now include parts of the South and North Rims and the bottom of the canyon by the Colorado River.

South Rim

Although more than 2,700 prehistoric Pueblo sites have been discovered in the Grand Canyon region, most are far from any roads and trails. Some are located on the tops of plateaus that were once part of the canyon's rims, but are now isolated "islands" in the desert, like the Powell Plateau seen from Pima and Hopi Point on the South Rim. One carefully excavated site, Tusayan, is located just a few miles east of Grand Canyon Village on the South Rim and is accessible by road. A visit here reveals glimpses of what life must have been like for a hamlet of about 30 ancestral Pueblo people, who lived here for about 20 years during the late 12th century. A self-guided walking tour of the site takes roughly one hour to complete. The site consists of an open plaza in the middle of a U-shaped pueblo where the villagers did their crafts, prepared their food, and engaged in many other activities, including racing, throwing, dolls, tops, darts, singing, and gambling. The people cooked, ate, and slept in second-story rooms with storage rooms along each side. Close by the plaza was a round, sunken structure known as a kiva, which was used as a village gathering place and ceremonial center. They enjoyed wearing fine jewelry and

"Descending Sheep" petroglyph panes *(detail)*, up Colorado River from Lees Ferry
Photo courtesy Grand Canyon National Park Museum Collection, #6185

"Descending Sheep" petroglyph panes *(detail)*, up Colorado River from Lees Ferry
Photo courtesy Grand Canyon National Park Museum Collection, #6185

clothing, which they probably secured from neighboring villages by trading their beautiful baskets and pottery.

North Rim

On the North Rim, the Walhalla Glades site was the summer home of a small farming village of about 20 people, who grew corn, beans, and squash, and returned to the canyon (probably to Unkar Delta) in winter. A "peninsula" surrounded on three sides by the Grand Canyon, Walhalla Glades has a lower elevation than most of the North Rim, allowing updrafts of warm air from the canyon to melt winter snows early. This made it a perfect spot for farming. Access is along the road to Cape Royal, with a one-mile hike down the Cliff Spring Trail. More than 100 farm sites have been found on Walhalla Glades, most with a one-room field house and agricultural terraces or garden plots. The site contains an ancestral Pueblo dwelling with nine rooms used for sleeping, eating, and storage. Additional food storage and processing was done in the Sky Island area, which is visible from the Walhalla Overlook. A good example of a granary storage room can be seen as you walk down the Cliff Springs Trail. There is a self-guided walking tour available at the site.

During the late 12th and early 13th centuries, the American Southwest suffered a series of droughts. The land could no longer support the agricultural demands of farming and a growing population. Eventually, the ancestral Pueblo people abandoned their villages and migrated south and east to the Hopi Mesas and the Rio Grande River Valley. Their culture evolved to become the modern-day Pueblo people—the Hopi and Pueblos of the Rio Grande Valley in New Mexico.

Inner Canyon

Inside the canyon below Lipan Point, the Unkar Delta is the site of numerous ancestral Pueblo dwellings dating from the 9th–early 12th century. Life along this area of alluvial terraces focused on farming, with early living sites built on the fertile terraces along Unkar Creek. As the population grew, living sites were moved to the slopes above the creek to make room for more crops. During the summer months, farming was probably done on the canyon's cooler, moister North Rim (Walhalla Glades) rather than the Unkar Delta. There is a self-guided loop trail that can be accessed by a trip on the river beginning at Lees Ferry. This tour through the past explores 13 individual family living and storage sites, as well as several larger pueblos above and along Unkar Creek.

For more information on ancestral Pueblo culture, visit the Tusayan Ruin and Museum (three miles west of Desert View, daily 9 A.M.–5 P.M., free admission). A self-guiding trail leads through the adjacent village remains.

"Descending Sheep" petroglyph panes *(detail),* up Colorado River from Lees Ferry
Photo courtesy Grand Canyon National Park Museum Collection, #6185

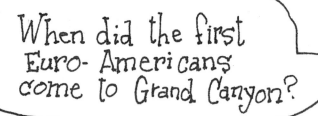

When did the first Euro-Americans come to Grand Canyon?

The year was 1540—Spaniard Francisco Vásquez de Coronado was leading a search for the mythic Seven Cities of Cibola in the southwestern United States. He sent a party northward under the command of García López de Cárdenas, whose small troop became the first Europeans to set eyes on the Grand Canyon. Their search for riches, however, proved futile, as they were unable to find a way across the great void of the canyon, thereby failing to find a valuable land or water route. They returned to Mexico with tales of a great canyon, with an unreachable river at its bottom.

The late 1500s saw the return of the Spanish to the region, not as explorers, but as colonists. By 1776, efforts were in full swing to convert the native peoples to Christianity and to extract tributes for the Spanish kingdom. One of these missionaries, Francisco Thomas Garces, traveling with Native American guides, reached the crimson cliffs of the western Grand Canyon near the outlet of Havasu Creek on the North Rim. After spending six days with the Havasupai, he followed a high and narrow cliff trail to a plateau covered with pinyon and juniper. There, he saw his first view of the Grand Canyon.

By the early 1800s, trappers and traders discovered that beavers were plentiful in Spanish-governed "New Spain" (Mexico, Arizona, New Mexico, California, Colorado, Utah). More opportunists flooded the area in 1821, with the opening of the Santa Fe Trail and its east-west trade routes. In 1848, much of the Southwest came under U.S. control after the war with Mexico. The U.S. government sent out teams of engineers to survey the new territories. One party leader, Lieutenant Joseph Christmas Ives, wrote, "Ours has been the first, and will doubtless be the last, party of whites to visit this profitless locality." Needless to say, his words were not prophetic!

John Wesley Powell
Photo courtesy Grand Canyon National Park Museum Collection

In 1869, John Wesley Powell, a one-armed Civil War veteran, led a team of four wooden boats and 10 men on a 1,000-mile Colorado River trip that went through the canyon—the first Euro-Americans to make the journey. His expeditions, and recent efforts to preserve natural resources and Native American rights, greatly influenced the future of the region.

That future proved to be a boom of visitors, homesteaders, and miners in the late 1800s. While geographers, artists, naturalists, photographers, and writers spread the word about a canyon "without rival upon the face of the globe," entrepreneurs were finding their niches. One homesteader was the infamous John D. Lee, a Mormon sent by the church to start the first ferry service across the upper Colorado River. Today, all river runners put in at Lees Ferry.

A slew of miners came to the Grand Canyon looking for profitable zinc, copper, lead, and asbestos mining claims; they included men like Cass Hite, John Hance, William Wallace Bass, Peter D. Berry, the Cameron brothers, Louis Boucher, and Daniel L. Hogan. Even though these mines never amounted to much, the prospectors soon found themselves tapping a different kind of resource: tourists.

Tau-Gu, Chief of the Paiutes, overlooking Virgin River with J. W. Powell
Photo courtesy Grand Canyon National Park Museum Collection

Are there historic buildings in Grand Canyon National Park?

There are a number of interesting historic structures along both rims and even down in the canyon itself, but most of them are located right in Grand Canyon Village. We've provided a walking map that reads from left to right, or west to east. All of the buildings described here are included in the Grand Canyon Village Historic District and are listed in the National Register of Historic Places.

1. Red Horse Station

Built in the 1890s and originally located 16 miles away, Red Horse Station was relocated to its present site in 1902 by Ralph Cameron. At that point it was renamed Cameron's Hotel and Camp. It served for a number of years as the terminus of the Flagstaff–Grand Canyon stage run and also as the village post office.

2. Kolb Studio

Between 1904 and 1926, the brothers Kolb—Ellsworth and Emery—built, altered, and added to this building. The brothers felt that there was a market among visitors for scenic photographs of the canyon, so they set up a photographic studio and photographed thousands of mule-ride passengers as they began their descent into the canyon. When riders returned several hours later, their portraits were ready for purchase. Today, prints of these photographs are available from the University of Northern Arizona Library.

3. Lookout Studio

Located on the edge of the Grand Canyon rim, Lookout Studio was designed by architect Mary Colter to resemble the stone structures built by Southwest Indians. The structure was built of native stone in 1914, providing a lounge and fireplace, as well as a room where postcards and artwork could be

Grand Canyon Village Historic District

② Kolb Studio
③ Lookout Studio
④ Bucky O'Neill Cabin
① Red Horse Station
⑤ Bright Angel Lodge
CANYON RIM
⑥ El Tovar Hotel
⑦ Hopi House
⑧ Verkamp Curios
⑨ Santa Fe Railway Station

purchased. Outside on the porch was a powerful telescope that allowed visitors to study details of the canyon.

4. Bucky O'Neill Cabin
Built in the 1890s, this is the oldest structure on the canyon rim and was the cabin of one of the Grand Canyon's most colorful characters. Bucky O'Neill was a prospector, politician, writer, lawman, and mayor of Prescott, Arizona. He served as a Rough Rider in the Spanish-American War with Teddy Roosevelt. He was killed the day before the famous charge up San Juan Hill.

5. Bright Angel Lodge
Another Mary Colter design, this property opened for business in 1935 to provide housing for budget-minded visitors. They could stay either in the lodge itself or in one of the cabins that cluster to the west of the lodge. Be sure to see the lounge's stone fireplace, which reflects the geologic strata of the canyon, from the Kaibab limestone at the canyon's rim, down to the river-worn stones at the bottom.

6. El Tovar Hotel
This 1905 masterpiece of a log-built structure was designed by architect Charles Whittlesey for the Santa Fe Railroad, which had just begun regular train service from Flagstaff to the canyon. In its early days, the El Tovar sported a barbershop, music room, solarium, bar, art room, and dining room.

7. Hopi House
Also completed in 1905, Hopi House was designed by Mary Colter, but in this case, most of the actual construction was done by Hopi Indians. After it was completed, a number of the Hopi lived in the building, creating rugs, basketry, and silver jewelry and giving visitors a glimpse of Hopi culture.

8. Verkamp's Curios
This is an offshoot of what was originally a souvenir shop operated by John Verkamp in 1898. In 1905, a big construction year in the village, he built his curio shop, and for many years after, the Verkamp family lived above the store. Today it is operated by Michael Verkamp, grandson of the store's founder.

9. Santa Fe Railway Station
Completed in 1909, this is one of only three log-constructed railway stations still in existence in the United States. The architect was Francis Wilson, and of his many commissions, this was his only log structure. Today, the station is the terminus for the Grand Canyon Railway, whose daily service was reinstated in the 1980s by Max and Thelma Biegert.

For additional reading, see *A Guide to the Grand Canyon Village Historic District* by Timothy Manns.

During the late 1840s, soldiers were some of the most adventuresome explorers of the Grand Canyon area. But it was a secondary role the army played—that of overseeing and paying for the Civilian Conservation Corps (CCC) camps in the 1930s—that helped transform the "big canyon" into the Grand Canyon that we know today.

The CCC, created by President Franklin D. Roosevelt in April 1933, was the first of the New Deal agencies and Roosevelt's favorite. Its mission was to accomplish simple work (not interfering with normal employment) confined to forestry, the prevention of soil erosion, flood control, and similar projects that conserved and developed the nation's natural resources. Roosevelt wrote, "This enterprise will pay dividends to the present and future generations. It will make improvements in national and state domains which have been largely forgotten in the past few years of industrial development.... More important, however, than the material gains will be the moral and spiritual value of such work." By the end of the CCC's eight years of operation, almost three million people had been put to work, at a total cost of $634 million.

Construction of River Trail by CCC enrollees
Photo courtesy Grand Canyon National Park Museum Collection, #3973c

Between 1933 and 1942, five companies of CCC workers (about 1,000 men) virtually transformed Grand Canyon National Park. During their tenure in the park, the CCC built or improved parts of the South Kaibab and Bright Angel Trails; most of Phantom Ranch; the Mile-and-a-Half, Three-Mile, Indian Garden, and Pipe Creek rest houses along the Bright Angel Trail; and the masonry walls that border all the lookout points and scenic turnouts. The CCC also was responsible for upgrading and maintaining trails throughout the park, carrying suspension cables for the Kaibab bridge down the Kaibab Trail to the river, building service roads, building the first trans-canyon telephone line, landscaping, cleaning ditches, and assembling service structures and cattle fences.

For many it was a labor of love, the benefits of which can still be found today in Grand Canyon National Park. For more information on the CCC at the Grand Canyon, pick up a copy of *The Ace in the Hole: A Brief History of Company 818 of the Civilian Conservation Corps* by Louis Lester Purvis.

The Grand Canyon Railway

On September 17, 1901, the first passenger train arrived at the South Rim via the Santa Fe Grand Canyon Railway. The rail line served for many years as a popular way to travel to the canyon. The beautiful Grand Canyon Depot was completed in 1910 and served as the arrival and departure point for all trains.

The heyday of this elegant way of travel faded as the popularity of the automobile grew, and in 1968 passenger train service to the Grand Canyon ceased. For many years the railbed sat unused, and the depot fell into decay. Then in 1987 Max and Thelma Biegert, who were in the

September 17, 1901: the first scheduled passenger train arrived at the Canyon from Williams, Arizona.
Photo courtesy Grand Canyon National Park Museum Collection, #2435

aviation business, collected the collateral on a delinquent loan: 22 miles of steel railroad track, part of the long-defunct Santa Fe Grand Canyon rail line. They decided to try to reintroduce rail service to the canyon. They acquired rail cars and two vintage steam engines and soon were running passenger train service to the canyon again from the Williams depot. By 1993 they were carrying over 100,000 passengers to the canyon and back each year, eliminating approximately 40,000 auto trips to the park. The 1.5-hour, one-way trip from Williams to the canyon covers 65 miles of scenic western landscape at 40 mph or less. The 1910 depot is now a National Historic Landmark and is still used to greet trains arriving at the canyon today.

The Grand Canyon Railway (800/843-8724, www.thetrain.com) runs historic excursion trains from Williams, Arizona, to the canyon daily except for December 24 and 25. These trains offer five classes of service departing Williams as early as 9 A.M. and arriving at the Grand Canyon at 11:15 A.M. For the return, trains depart at 3 P.M. and arrive back in Williams at 5:15 P.M. Prices range from $65–170 for adults, $40–145 for youth 11–16, and $30–95 for children 2–10. Prices depend on level of class and are subject to change. Overnight packages are available.

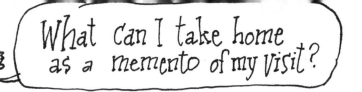

What can I take home as a memento of my visit?

With an awe-inspiring backdrop like the Grand Canyon, anyone with a camera can take home some of the magic without stealing anything away from the beauty of the park. There are no mementos quite like the photographs that capture your own special memories, such as a dip in the pools in front of Havasu Falls, a walk through a meadow of wildflowers near Uncle Jim Trail, or a view of the sunrise from Imperial Point.

For less personal keepsakes, check out the park shops, galleries, and museums. Besides the ever-popular T-shirts and mugs, there is a wide range of gifts that evoke the spirit of the Grand Canyon. These include hand-wrought gold and silver jewelry made by world-renowned artists from the Hopi, Zuni, Navajo, and Santa Domingo tribes; basketry crafted by Hopi, Paiute, Navajo, and Papago artisans; Hopi-carved Kachina Dolls; Navajo rugs; minerals, petrified wood, and fossils; authentic Indian pottery; moccasins, jackets, and leather goods; and paintings of the Grand Canyon that range in price $300–1,800.

The search for natural souvenirs can become a problem in the Grand Canyon. That's why people are prohibited from destroying or removing just about everything in the park, including plants, driftwood, animals, antlers, minerals, and especially any archaeological artifacts. The canyon's fragile archaeological resources provide important and tangible links to the area's history and must remain a part of the park's archaeological record. That's why a family driving out of the canyon with a pile of rocks shouldn't be surprised if the ranger hands over a $50–100 citation—one of the less desirable of Grand Canyon mementos. These regulations are designed to keep the canyon intact, despite the nearly five million visitors per year who want to take a piece of it home.

III
Getting Around

Decisions..
Decisions..

◄ AIR TOURS

SHUTTLE BUS STOP ►

◄ MOTORCOACH TOURS

{ BICYCLE RENTAL ►

◄ HIKING TRAILS

PARK AUTO ROUTES ►

◄ TAXI SERVICE

MULE RIDES ►

◄ RIVER TRIPS

NATURE STUDY TRIPS ►

• WINTER •
◄ CROSS-COUNTRY SKIING
SNOWSHOEING

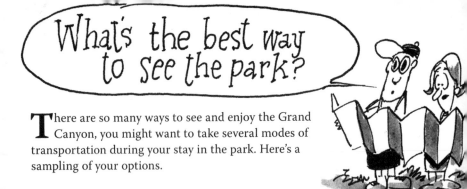

What's the best way to see the park?

There are so many ways to see and enjoy the Grand Canyon, you might want to take several modes of transportation during your stay in the park. Here's a sampling of your options.

Walking

Year-round, the best way to escape the crowds and see the Grand Canyon is to hoof it—walking, hiking, or backpacking some of the more than 33 miles of maintained trails within the park boundaries. You can take these trails along the rims or down into the canyon. Hikes range from easy walks along the North and South Rims to view the canyon from scenic lookout points, to steeper treks into the canyon and remote backcountry areas. Remember that even the relatively flat Rim Trail along Hermit Road, which is paved between Yavapai Point and Maricopa Point and unpaved on to Hermits Rest, can be dangerous—especially near the cliff edges. And, although the scenic viewpoints have guardrails, they're not childproof. You'll need to assess your limits before setting out on one of the Inner Canyon journeys. Don't forget to bring lots of water, snacks, and extra clothes in case of a sudden change in weather. The Grand Canyon is desert country, with intense heat during the summer. Read up on backcountry regulations and safety. It's a good idea to stop at the nearest visitor center or ranger station for an update on trail closures and conditions before you start.

Shuttle Bus

Year-round, the park provides a free shuttle service for visitors on the South Rim, with no tickets required. Taking the shuttle, combined with a few short walks, is a great way to view the canyon and enjoy the scenery along the way. Currently, the shuttle follows three loop routes: Kaibab Trail Route, Village Route, and Hermits Rest Route. The shuttle makes frequent stops that are clearly marked along the way. Currently, the Kaibab Trail Route shuttle departs daily every 15 minutes 6:30 A.M.–5 P.M. and every 30 minutes 5:15–6:30 A.M. and 5–7:45 P.M. This route goes from the Canyon View Information Plaza to Yaki Point, with stops at the South Kaibab Trailhead and Pipe Creek Vista along the way. If you want to stay on the bus for the entire loop, you should plan on 30 minutes. The Village Route shuttle runs daily every 15 minutes 6:30 A.M.–7:30 P.M. and every 30 minutes 5:15–6:30 A.M. and 7:30–10 P.M. This route travels between the Yavapai Observation Station, Canyon View Information Plaza, hotels, restaurants, campgrounds, and other facilities in the Village area. Allow 60 minutes to travel the entire loop without getting off the bus. The Hermits Rest Route shuttle runs every 15 minutes 9:30 A.M.–sunset; every 30 minutes 5:15–9:30 A.M. and sunset to one hour after sunset. This route goes between Hermits Rest, Hopi Point, and Trailview Overlook with several stops in between. Check *The Guide* for pick-up and drop-off times at each stop. There is no shuttle to Desert View, nor is there a shuttle on the North Rim of the Grand Canyon.

Taxi
Daily, 24-hour service is available to the Grand Canyon Airport, trail-heads, and other destinations. Call Grand Canyon Taxi (928/638-2822 or 928/638-2631, ext. 6563), which is run by Xanterra. No taxi service is available on the North Rim.

Driving
During our peak season (April–October), you will be sharing our limited driving roads with lots of other traffic. You'll also be competing for parking spaces, which is often the most challenging part of any visit to the canyon during peak times. When you can, take the shuttle to avoid parking head-aches. Both rims of the canyon experience storms and freezing temperatures. Summer thunderstorms may be brief, but they can make driving dangerous, with fierce hail and lightning. It's a good idea to call for current road information (928/638-7888) before you arrive at the park.

Bicycling
You can bike all of the paved roads open to private vehicles, plus the restricted Hermit Road, but beware of motorists who may not be aware of you. Biking here is not for novice riders. You need to be in good shape and pay close attention to auto traffic because shoulders are narrow to nonexistent along roadways. Bicycles are not allowed on any park trails except for the Greenway Trail, and bicyclists must obey all traffic regulations in the park. They should always ride with the flow of traffic. In the winter, snow and narrower roads create challenging biking conditions, while spring and fall are the best times for riding. Consider riding at first light to avoid heavy traffic and hot temperatures. Bicycles are not available for rent inside the park—the closest bicycle rentals, parts, and repairs are available in the towns of Flagstaff and Sedona, Arizona, south of the park.

Motorcoach Tours
Narrated motorcoach tours of the South Rim are available year-round via Xanterra Parks and Resorts (303/297-2757 or 888/297-2757, reserve-gcsr@xanterra.com, www.grandcanyonlodges.com). These tours include trips

along Hermit Road to Hermits Rest (two hours, $18.25 per person) and along Desert View Drive to Desert View (3.75 hours, $31.50 per person). For spectacular views of the sun rising and setting over the canyon, take a Sunrise or Sunset Tour (1.5 hours, $14.50 per person), which stops at various scenic lookouts along the way. You can take a combination of any two tours for a special price of $40 per person. Children 16 and under are free on all tours when accompanied by a paying adult.

There are no concessioner-operated motorcoach tours of the North Rim. The Grand Canyon Railway (800/843-8724, www.thetrain.com) also offers narrated motorcoach tours along Hermit Road and Desert View Drive, in combination with the Grand Canyon Railway train trip, for an additional fee. (For information on the Grand Canyon Railway, see *How do we get there?* in the *Getting There* chapter.)

Mule Trips

Xanterra Parks and Resorts (303/297-2757 or 888/297-2757, reserve-gcsr@ xanterra.com, www.grandcanyonlodges.com) offers a one-day mule trip below the South Rim in the canyon. The seven-hour trip descends to Plateau Point along the Bright Angel Trail and includes lunch ($148.35 per person). You can also book an overnight mule trip to Phantom Ranch ($401.16 for the first person, less for additional people), including box lunch and accommodations at the Ranch. During the winter months, a three-day/two-night trip to Phantom Ranch is available. Rider restrictions apply for all trips. Along the North Rim, you have a several mule trip choices, offered by Canyon Trail Rides (P.O. Box 128, Tropic, Utah 84776, 435/679-8665, www.canyonrides.com). These include a one-hour Rim Ride ($30), a half-day ride to Uncle Jim's Point ($65), a half-day trip to Supai Tunnel in the canyon ($65), or a one-day trip to Roaring Springs in the canyon ($125).

River Trips

If you're looking for more relaxation than adventure, try the half-day, smooth-water raft trips offered by Colorado River Discovery (888/522-6644, www .raftthecanyon.com) starting in Page, Arizona. These trips, running March 1–November 30 of each year, are great for the entire family (kids aged 4 and up can join you). Adult fare is $76, and children 4–11 are $66, water or soda is provided on your trip. The company also offers a full-day row trip on Mondays, Wednesdays, and Sundays March–May and September–November. The day begins at 8 A.M., with a return at 5 P.M. Fees includes lunch and are $161 for adults and $151 for kids. For longer trips on the river, you can contact one of the many commercial concessionaires (see *Licensed Outfitters* in the *Quick Reference* chapter) who guide all levels of river trips down the Colorado.

Air Tours

Both fixed-wing and helicopter scenic air tours of the Grand Canyon region are offered daily from sites outside of the park. Some air operators also fly to the Grand Canyon Airport from Phoenix/Scottsdale, Arizona or Las Vegas, Nevada. For a list of air tour operators, contact the Grand Canyon Chamber of Commerce (P.O. Box 3007, Grand Canyon, AZ 86023, 888/472-2696, www. grandcanyonchamber.org) or see the *Telephone and Website Directory* in the *Quick Reference* chapter.

Cross-country Skiing and Snowshoeing

During the winter (November–March), the national forest lands around the park offer limited backcountry trails for cross-country skiers and snowshoers. On the South Rim, you can ski around the Kaibab National Forest, where you may find groomed trails near Grandview Point. Call the Tusayan Ranger Station (928/638-2443) for more information. On the North Rim, you can again try Kaibab National Forest lands. You may even be able to ski to park boundaries on the Jacob Lake Road once it's closed for the season. For more information, call the North Kaibab Ranger Station (928/643-7395).

Nature Study Trips and Field Courses

The Grand Canyon Field Institute (928/638-2485 or 866/471-4435, www. grandcanyon.org/fieldinstitute) offers year-round short field courses on all aspects of life at the Grand Canyon. Activities range from classroom presentations to hiking, horsepacking, and river-rafting and river-running in the park. Most courses last 2–5 days, with tuition varying from $425 for hiking and journal-keeping in the Grand Canyon and $415 for a three-day yoga class to $655 for an eight-day backpacking loop.

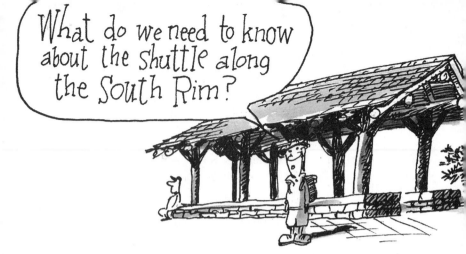

What do we need to know about the shuttle along the South Rim?

First of all, you need to make sure that you get on the bus that's going to your desired destination. That's easy: Currently, all you have to do is read the name or colored square on the front of each white, brown-and-tan, or white-with-green-stripes bus. The name will indicate one of the following routes: Village Route, Hermits Rest Route, or Kaibab Trail Route. Don't worry if you "just" missed a shuttle bus; another one will be coming by your stop soon. Enjoy the scenery while you wait.

The shuttle makes frequent stops that are clearly marked along the way. Currently, the Kaibab Trail Route shuttle departs daily every 15 minutes 6:30 A.M.–5 P.M. and every 30 minutes 5:15–6:30 A.M. and 5–7:45 P.M. This route goes from the Canyon View Information Plaza to Yaki Point, with stops at the South Kaibab Trailhead and Pipe Creek Vista along the way. If you want to stay on the bus for the entire loop, you should plan on 30 minutes. The Village Route shuttle runs daily every 15 minutes 6:30 A.M.–7:30 P.M. and every 30 minutes 5:15–6:30 A.M. and 7:30–10 P.M. This route travels between the Yavapai Observation Station, Canyon View Information Plaza, hotels, restaurants, campgrounds, and other facilities in the Village area. Allow 60 minutes to travel the entire loop without getting off the bus. The Hermits Rest Route shuttle runs every 15 minutes 9:30 A.M.–sunset and every 30 minutes 5:15–9:30 A.M. and sunset to one hour after sunset. This route goes between Hermits Rest, Hopi Point, and Trailview Overlook with several stops in between. Check *The Guide* for pick-up and drop-off times at each stop. There is no shuttle to Desert View, nor is there a shuttle on the North Rim of the Grand Canyon.

It's important to know the rules for riding the shuttles. Pets are not allowed on the buses, except for service animals for visitors with disabilities. Most shuttle buses are not wheelchair accessible. An accessibility permit is available for private vehicle use in any shuttle-only area. Ask at the entrance gates, Canyon View Information Plaza, or the North Rim Visitor Center about this permit. To reserve a wheelchair-accessible shuttle, you need to make arrangements at least 24 hours in advance by calling 928/638-0591.

Lastly, some words of advice to shuttle riders. Water is not available along the West Rim, except at the last stop, Hermits Rest. It's a good idea to take a canteen or water bottle. In addition, we have thunder and lightning storms, which can be a hazard. My advice is to stay away from exposed rim areas, like the lookout points, during our storms. You should always be prepared for a sudden rainstorm, especially during the summer. Take a raincoat or poncho with you on the shuttle. Finally, if you decide to walk between some of the shuttle stops (a great idea), remember to walk only along the Rim Trail. Our shuttles take up most of the road, leaving little room for pedestrians. Don't forget, there is no shuttle along the North Rim—you're on your own there.

Where are the East and West Rim Drives?

Throughout this book we have referred to the South and North Rims of the Grand Canyon. When we refer to the East and West Rims, that doesn't mean that the canyon is square. The explanation is simple. There's a road that runs along the South Rim of the canyon, and it runs in an east/west direction from Desert View to Hermits Rest. This rim road intersects with the south entrance road at Grand Canyon Village. Desert View Drive (or, as it was previously known, East Rim Drive) is the road from Desert View, at the east end of the rim road, west to the intersection with the south entrance road. Hermit Road (or West Rim Drive) runs from the West Rim Interchange near the Bright Angel Lodge to Hermits Rest; this is the westernmost point accessible by paved road on the South Rim. Separating the two roads is the community known as Grand Canyon Village.

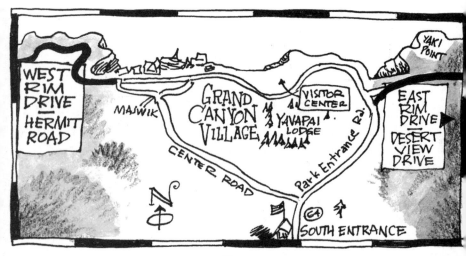

Can we drive to most sights?

Yes and no. It depends on what area of the park you're exploring. Let's take a look at both rims of the canyon for the answers.

South Rim

Yes, you can drive to the parking areas of most lookouts on the East Rim, including Grandview Point and trailhead, Moran Point, Lipan Point, Navajo Point, and Desert View. Most lookouts do require easy walks, some longer than others. No, you can't drive to the road to Hermits Rest, South Kaibab Trailhead, and Yaki Point off Desert View Drive because they're closed to commercial and private vehicles.

Although you may be able to see the Rim Trail around the hotels and restaurants in Grand Canyon Village, you can't actually drive along it. The only way to see this three-mile stretch of the South Rim is to hoof it. You might want to start or end this jaunt at one of the many eating spots along the Rim Trail. Parking will be your only headache.

North Rim

Yes, from May 15 to the first snow (usually late October–mid-November), you can drive to many viewpoints on the North Rim, including the Grand Canyon Lodge, Point Imperial, Cape Royal, Vista Encantada, Roosevelt Point, Walhalla Overlook, and the Indian Country exhibit and lookout. Two of the most spectacular vistas along this rim, Bright Angel Point and Angel's Window, require quarter-mile walks that are relatively easy but may seem more difficult because of the higher elevation of the North Rim.

No, you can't drive to anyplace on the North Rim beginning with the first snow. That's because the average precipitation (much of it snowfall) on the North Rim is about 26 inches annually. Once the Arizona Department of Transportation closes Highway 67 south of Jacob Lake for the winter season, the North Rim is also closed to vehicle traffic.

Keep in mind that the park occupies an area about the size of the state of Delaware. Much of this area is roadless, but there are unmaintained dirt roads. Before venturing on any of these roads, check at the nearest ranger station or information office. Many cross restricted lands.

How can we get from the South to the North rim?

By Automobile

Even though it's a mere 10 miles across the canyon as the raven flies, the drive between the North and South Rims takes about five hours (220 miles). The roads that connect the South with the North Rim include Highways 64, 89, and 89A. Most of this drive is on a two-lane road with heavy traffic through the Navajo Indian Reservation. As the road descends from the South Rim east to Cameron, the landscape changes from woodland to blackbrush. You'll pass the Little Colorado River Overlook about 20 miles east of the park's east entrance. There is a spectacular view beyond the group of curio shops. The road is narrow and slippery when wet, but you can walk to the view-point. As you head north from Cameron, Highway 89 skirts the western edge of the Painted Desert, then follows the base of the Echo Cliffs for 60 miles. At Bitter Springs you'll get onto Highway 89A to Navajo Bridge, which crosses the Colorado River. Be sure to stop at the parking area on the north side and walk out onto the old bridge for a great view of Marble Canyon. The road then skirts the base of the Vermilion Cliffs for about 25 miles. Look for soaring condors. At House Rock, you'll begin to gain altitude, as the road rises into a large ponde-rosa pine forest. At Jacob Lake, Highway 67 goes 32 miles south to the boundary of the North Rim of the Grand Canyon. You'll be able to find food, fuel, and lodging at both Cameron and Jacob Lake but precious little in between. Because this route can be icy and snowpacked in the winter, it's best to call ahead for road conditions (Arizona 888/411-7623, Grand Canyon 928/638-7888).

By Trans-Canyon Shuttle

Between mid-May and mid-October, there is a trans-canyon shuttle service (928/638-2820) that provides daily transportation between the South and the North Rims. The shuttle bus leaves the North Rim at 7 A.M. and arrives at the South Rim at 11:30 A.M. It departs the South Rim at 1:30 P.M. and arrives at the North Rim at 6 P.M. Fare per person is $70 one-way, $130 round-trip, with special rates for 10 or more people. Reservations are required. Call the service directly, or contact one of the lodging transportation desks.

By Hiking

There are a few hearty souls who actually hike across the canyon from rim to rim. It's a strenuous, three-day, 21-mile trek along the North and South Kaibab Trails and requires top physical conditioning and stamina. At one point, the trail crosses the Colorado River via a narrow footbridge 70 feet above the water. For obvious reasons, this hike is not meant for most visitors.

That's because the Grand Canyon is the only national park in the country to have a K–12 school system. (The graduating class usually has about 20 students.) Actually, we have an entire community of year-round residents in the South Rim area, who help keep the park running all year long.

The Grand Canyon School serves about 380 students. These students are from the families of National Park Service staff, concession workers, and other personnel who call the Grand Canyon home. During weekday school hours (Mon.–Thurs. 7:55 A.M.–4:15 P.M.), it's not unusual to see yellow school buses driving the roads throughout the South Rim, picking up or dropping off students near their homes. There's even a summer school that usually runs the first six weeks of summer vacation. Even though we're in a national park, all driving rules apply for our school buses, as they would in any other part of the country. If a school bus is stopped in front of you or has its lights flashing, do not attempt to pass. In front of the school, between the south entrance road and Grand Canyon Village on the South Rim, you must obey the 15 mph speed limit when school is in session.

In addition to a school system, we also have services for our year-round residents as well as visitors, including a clinic and pharmacy, a dentist, a general store, a bank, a post office, an auto repair shop, child care services, and a radio station (KSGC 92.1 FM). Yep, it's a regular ol' little town, with about 1,200 residents in peak season.

hat's a tricky question. Some visitors say that they saw the entire park in three days (it's possible). For others, it takes a lifetime to really know the park—and even then it has surprises. The best advice I can give on the subject is to read up on the Grand Canyon and then decide what you want to see in the amount of time you have. But don't rush your visit here. You have to take into account the rough and unforgiving terrain, the exhausting heat of our summer months, and the amount of traffic and visitors you'll encounter during your visit to the park. Here are some of my suggestions on ways to see the park in the amount of time you have.

Two Days

If you have two days to spend at the Grand Canyon, I would suggest staying on the South Rim. You can begin your visit by touring the West and East Rims (by shuttle, by motorcoach tour, or by combining these with a few walks along the Rim Trail). You can add to your knowledge of this place by taking a walking tour of the buildings in the historic district of Grand Canyon Village, visiting the Tusayan Museum and Ruin along Desert View (East Rim) Drive, or joining a ranger-led walk or talk. If you feel up to it, you could take a short hike into the canyon along the Bright Angel or South Kaibab Trails or a longer (six-hour) mule ride to Plateau Point in the canyon. Don't forget to enjoy the many dining options along the rim, including breakfast at the El Tovar Hotel and dinner at the Arizona Room near the Bright Angel Lodge. To make your South Rim excursion a really memorable one, make sure you watch a sunrise or sunset over the canyon. Then, on your next visit to the Grand Canyon, you can explore the North Rim.

Three Days

If you have three days to spend, and you want to see both the North and South Rims, then you'll have to pick from the South Rim activities above so that they fit into 1.5 days. Be sure you have advance room reservations or a campsite reserved at the Jacob Lake Campground. Then, you can drive to the North Rim (five hours straight through), making stops to see Desert View, Cameron, the Navajo Indian Reservation, Lees Ferry, and many scenic areas along the way. With stops, the drive could take you 6–7 hours. That will leave you one day to see the North Rim. You can spend some time touring the rim by taking a short walk to Bright Angel Point and other easy access trails, including Cliff Springs and Cape Royal. You can take a drive along the Cape Royal Road to Point Imperial and other scenic lookout points. You can make a visit to Walhalla Glades Ruins along a self-guided trail. Make sure to take advantage of the dining opportunities at the Grand Canyon Lodge, and don't forget to watch the sunrise from Point Imperial.

If you have more time to spend at the Grand Canyon, and you feel up to the task, I would suggest several day hikes along the rims or into the canyon or an overnight trek or multiday adventure into some of the canyon's more remote areas, like the village of Supai in the western Grand Canyon. Don't forget to make advance room reservations in Supai Village.

Can we take a walk with a ranger?

Let's go!

Year-round on the South Rim and May 15–October 15 on the North Rim, you can join a ranger and get the inside scoop on the many facets of this amazing place. Many ranger-led programs include short hikes into the canyon, as you learn about the history and geology around you. You can join a ranger to explore the fossil world inside the rock layers of the canyon, watch a sunset, or learn about the human history of the region. Kids can also join Junior Ranger activities. To find out more about programs occurring during your visit, check out *The Guide* newspaper (South or North Rim editions) for times and locations.

Each evening, rangers give programs that explore the many aspects of the Grand Canyon. These programs include slide and video presentations. On the South Rim, evening programs are held June–September in Mather Amphitheater, located behind the Park Headquarters. (Be sure to dress warmly.) From late September to mid-May, they're held in the Shrine of Ages building next to the visitor center at the west end of Parking Lot A. These programs are always entertaining and informative, and they're free.

At Desert View, rangers present programs on the Tusayan Ruin, an ancestral Pueblo village. From May to October, you can join a ranger for a fascinating guided walk through these ruins. You can also join a ranger for a special sunset walk and viewing at beautiful Desert View Point. For more information, check *The Guide* for more details.

On the North Rim, rangers offer daily talks and walks about geology, human history, and wildlife. Evening campfire programs are presented in the campground amphitheater. Afternoon Lodge talks are also very entertaining and cover a variety of topics.

Notable Grand Canyon Architects

Charles Whittlesey: El Tovar Hotel (1905)

Francis Wilson: Santa Fe Grand Canyon Railroad Depot Building (1909)

Gilbert Underwood: Grand Canyon (North Rim) Lodge (1928)

Mary Elizabeth Jane Colter:
  Hopi House (1905)
  Lookout Studio (1914)
  Hermits Rest (1914)
  Phantom Ranch (1922)
  Desert View Watchtower (1932)
  Bright Angel Lodge (1935)
  Fred Harvey Men's Dormitory (1936)
  Colter Hall (1937)

Mary Colter at age 23 making a pottery bowl
Photo courtesy: Grand Canyon National Park Museum Collection #16952

Can we ride a mule into the Canyon?

Yes, you can still ride a mule to the canyon floor. It's easier than hiking, and it gives you a chance to take your eyes off the trail and enjoy spectacular views during the descent.

Mule trips into the Grand Canyon have been offered since the 1880s, with the opening of the Bright Angel Trail. The saddle trips became so popular by the 1920s that Phantom Ranch was built in 1922 to accommodate the mule train guests. A distinction to remember is that you're on a mule—a cross between a horse and a donkey—not a donkey. Mules were bred as pack animals, with the ability to carry up to 200 pounds each, while the much smaller donkeys were bred for lighter domestic work. There are a few rules to follow—riders must not weigh more than 200 pounds, must be at least 4 feet, 7 inches in height, must be able to speak and understand fluent English, be in good physical condition, cannot be pregnant, and should not be afraid of heights or large animals.

South Rim

There are two types of mule trips you can make into the canyon from the South Rim. One-day mule trips to Plateau Point depart daily year-round from the stone corral at the head of Bright Angel Trail. The ride descends about 3,200 feet to the Tonto Platform and Plateau Point, where you can see the Colorado River 1,320 feet below. This approximately seven-hour round trip costs $148.35 per person (prices subject to change), which includes tax and a box lunch. Other trips from the South Rim include an overnight to Phantom Ranch on Bright Angel Creek, where riders spend the night in ranch cabins and start the next day with a home-cooked breakfast. Lunch and steak dinner are also included. The first day's 10.5-mile ride takes 5.5 hours, followed by a 7.3-mile, 4.5-hour trek on day two. Rides depart daily year-round from the stone corral at the head of Bright Angel Trail. Cost is $401.16 for the first person or two for $709.46, with each additional person costing $321.11. There is also a two-night ride that runs $945.68 for parties of two, with prices varying depending upon the number of people.

For all of the popular South Rim mule trips, you'll need to make reservations well in advance with Xanterra Parks and Resorts (303/297-2757 or

888/297-2757, reserve-gcsr@xanterra.com, www.grandcanyonlodges.com). You can call up to 13 months before your arrival date. If you're in the park and do not have reservations, call Xanterra South Rim (928/638-2631) or check at the Bright Angel Transportation Desk around 7 A.M. for cancellations or to be put on the waiting list.

North Rim

On the less-visited North Rim, you can still ride a mule into the canyon—you just have fewer choices. A bonus is that the rides, offered by Canyon Trail Rides (P.O. Box 128, Tropic, Utah 84776, 435/679-8665, www.canyonrides. com), cost less than on the South Rim. If you just have a bit of time, try their one-hour ride on the canyon rim for $30. Half-day trips ($65) depart from the Grand Canyon Lodge daily during the season (May–October) at 7:30 A.M. and 12:30 P.M. Riders must be a minimum of 10 years old. On this trip, you'll descend 2,400 feet into the canyon to Uncle Jim's Point or take an alternate trip to Supai Tunnel on the North Kaibab Trail. A full-day trip ($125) also starts from the Lodge and descends 4,500 feet to Roaring Springs, where you'll enjoy lunch before your return.

Two women and a mule ascending Bright Angel Trail, 1910
Photo courtesy Grand Canyon National Park Museum Collection, #5433

Are there any self-guided tours of the Grand Canyon?

If you want to be your own guide, you have a variety of trails to choose from, in all areas of the park. This is a great way to view the sights and set your own pace. If you have questions after you've taken a self-guided tour, you can either join a ranger-led walk or simply ask a ranger your questions by visiting a visitor center or information station on either rim.

South Rim

There is a great self-guided walking tour of buildings that are designated landmarks in the historic district of Grand Canyon Village. On this easy 1.5-mile tour, you'll be able to visit nine historic buildings: 1) the Santa Fe Railway Station; 2) El Tovar Hotel; 3) Hopi House; 4) Verkamp's Curios; 5) Bright Angel Lodge; 6) Bucky O'Neill's Cabin; 7) Lookout Studio; 8) Kolb Studio; and 9) Red Horse Station. Depending on how long you want to stay at each building, this tour could take you 1–2 hours. A word of warning: Some of the stairs between these buildings are steep, and you may require assistance.

You can also create your own self-guided tour by walking along the nine-mile Rim Trail, stopping at lookout points and interpretive signs along the way. Restrooms are available at Bright Angel Lodge and El Tovar Hotel.

Another interesting site on the South Rim that can be explored by self-guided tour is the Grand Canyon Cemetery, located just west of the Shrine of Ages building. The cemetery has 304 plots reserved for people who have contributed greatly to the park, like early settlers, prospectors, trail guides, and government officials, as well as people who have worked in the park and their immediate families. As you walk among the headstones, you'll read names like John Hance, W. W. Bass, Pete Berry, Ralph Cameron, the Kolb brothers, John Verkamp, and Gunnar Widforss. There is even a memorial to the 128 passengers killed in the 1956 collision of United and TWA airliners that occurred 20,000 feet above the canyon.

The Tusayan Museum and Ruins located along Desert View (East Rim) Drive (a 30-minute drive from Grand Canyon Village) provides visitors with a wonderful opportunity to explore the site of an 800-year-old ancestral pueblo. After you walk through the settlement site, you can visit the museum, which displays many of the artifacts uncovered during the excavation of the site in the 1930s.

North Rim

Along this rim you can take several easy self-guided walks. Here are some highlights:

- Pick up a brochure from the Grand Canyon Lodge or the log shelter located in the parking lot of the lodge, and enjoy a 0.5-mile (round-trip) self-guided nature walk along the Bright Angel Point Trail.

- The Widforss Trail starts from the parking lot just off the park entrance road, two miles north of Grand Canyon Lodge. The first 2.5 miles of this trail is an easy self-guided tour with brochures located at the trailhead.

- There is a wonderful 0.8-mile self-guided loop tour of the Walhalla Glades Ruin, an ancestral Pueblo farming site located off the Cape Royal Road on the North Rim. With the walking tour brochure (found in a dispenser box at the site), you can explore 13 different sites, including living and farming areas that wind over alluvial terraces and drainages. Allow at least 45 minutes for the round-trip tour.

- The half-mile Cape Royal Trail begins at the southeast side of the Cape Royal parking lot. Take this self-guided trail a little more than a quarter of a mile, and you will arrive at Angels Window and the Cape Royal Overlook, with a spectacular view of the Colorado River.

How can we avoid the crowds?

There is one simple trick to avoiding the throngs of Grand Canyon visitors: Don't come in the summer. However, if summer is your only vacation opportunity, the next best thing is to walk along the North Rim or South Rim or down a canyon trail—anywhere other than the teeming South Rim Village area. Since most of our visitors stay on the main South Rim Trail, you can lose the crowd by taking the less-frequented North Rim trails or the South Rim trails that descend into the canyon. Some of the shorter South Rim trails (less than 10 miles) include South Kaibab Trail to Cedar Ridge (three miles round-trip) and Bright Angel Trail to Indian Garden (nine miles round-trip). Some of our wilderness trails aren't as regularly maintained and might require some route-finding skills due to washouts and large boulders. If you're up for this kind of experience, try Grandview Trail to Horseshoe Mesa (six miles round-trip, steep and narrow) or Hermit Trail to Santa Maria Springs (five miles round-trip, steep and narrow). On the North Rim, you can try the self-guiding Bright Angel Point Trail (0.5 mile round-trip), Cape Royal Trail (0.6 mile round-trip), Cliff Springs Trail (one mile round-trip), Transept Trail (three miles round-trip), Widforss Point (10 miles round-trip), and the historic Uncle Jim Trail (five miles round-trip).

No matter where you hike, be sure to check at a visitor center for current trail conditions and closures. Things to bring along include a comfortable daypack, one gallon of water per person on hot days, snacks, layered clothing, walking or hiking shoes or boots, a hat and shirt to shield you from the sun, a first-aid kit, a flashlight (in case you don't get back to the rim before dark), a map, and a compass. Lastly, but most importantly, make sure you pick a trail that matches your stamina and won't aggravate any past injuries. For more information about hiking the Grand Canyon, refer to the *Recreational Opportunities* chapter of this book.

What are the best spots and best times to take pictures?

That's easy at a place like the Grand Canyon, where the sun shines bright all day and almost every spot offers scenic vistas.

The best times to take photos are mornings and evenings, when the sun is low in the sky and shadows add dimension and atmosphere to your pictures. Try to avoid mid-day shots, when the normally brilliant colors of the canyon appear to be washed out by the sun's rays. If you can, let clouds add drama to your photographs. Thunderstorms that hit the canyon during July and August offer particularly good opportunities to capture the dramatic buildup of storm clouds, as well as the aftermath of rain-soaked canyon vistas.

It's a little harder to advise you on the best places to take your photos, but here are some quick suggestions. Try a sunrise shot at Yaki, Mather, Lipan, or Yavapai Points. For a shot of the Colorado River, try a telephoto lens from Desert View, Pima, Hopi, Mohave, Yavapai, Moran, and Lipan Points. You can take a chance on getting some shots under a full moon over the canyon or a lightning storm at night, but you'll need a tripod or solid rest for an exposure of about 1–10 seconds or more. Photos of animals at the canyon are best taken in the early morning or evening, around the ponderosa pine forests near Grand Canyon Village and at the North Rim. Wildflowers and flowering cacti start blooming in the canyon in early spring, especially in hanging gardens at seeps and around the river. North Rim wildflowers begin their season in April, and South Rim wildflowers begin their season in June. Finally, you can photograph many interesting rock formations in the canyon; for a better picture, zoom in on the formation of your choice to isolate it.

Check *The Guide* for summer digital photography workshops. Usually, in July, Canon and the American Park Network presents free 1–2 hour digital photography workshops. Professional photographers lead photo walks beginning at the El Tovar Hotel and share their experiences taking landscape and wildlife photographs. A 45-minute evening slideshow generally follows the workshop.

How do the seasons affect getting around in the park?

The really big change around here happens in the winter, when the park becomes much less crowded and opens its arms to the many animals that are year-round residents.

South Rim

The roads all around the South Rim can be icy or covered in snow, so driving around the park becomes more hazardous. At night, it's not unusual to experience freezing temperatures that will make you wish you had brought your long johns to the Grand Canyon. Winter is quite a wonderful time around here, as the crowds have thinned out, the daytime weather is fairly moderate, and there is a special majesty to the canyon when viewed under late afternoon light. Most of the South Rim visitor services are open for business, while a few close up shop until summer.

North Rim

During the winter, the road to the North Rim closes, and most of this part of the park is closed to visitors. There are a few winter guests who snowshoe or cross-country ski into the North Rim and then hike across the canyon, but they're rare. The North Rim in the winter is even more remote and quiet than it is during the rest of the year. Although there are no services within park boundaries, visitors can still find gas, food, and lodging in Jacob Lake and Fredonia, Arizona, as well as Kanab and St. George, Utah.

Inner Canyon

During the winter months, the temperature in the canyon is at its best, with no intense heat during the day and only an occasional freeze during the night. Winter is a time when you're more likely to see canyon animals enjoying their habitat, without the scorching daytime summer temperatures.

IV

Lodging and Dining

After a day of walking a rim trail or riding a mule to Plateau Point, a shower and a comfortable bed can be a great way to end the day. From May 15 to October 15, you have quite a few lodgings to choose from. There are nearly 1,480 overnight accommodations in nine lodgings (eight inside the park, and one at the park's south entrance).

Year-round, you can pick from almost as many accommodations on the South Rim and at Phantom Ranch in the canyon. Rooms range from rustic cabins without baths to a suite in the El Tovar Hotel. Advance reservations at any of the Grand Canyon National Park Lodges are available through Xanterra reservations (303/297-2757 or 888/297-2757, www.grandcanyon-lodges.com). If you're in the park and you haven't made reservations, you can always take a chance and check with any of the lodging desks about last-minute cancellations, or call Xanterra South Rim (928/638-2631). Although visitors do cancel their reservations from time to time, this is not a recommended way to find a place to stay in the park. Remember, if you want your first choice, make your reservations up to 23 months in advance, especially for the summer season. (All rates listed below are subject to change.)

South Rim

Built by the Fred Harvey Company in 1905, the **El Tovar Hotel** is the architectural crown jewel of the Grand Canyon, a work of art along the rim designed to complement the pinyon pine landscape that surrounds it as well as the natural beauty of the canyon. The hotel is a National Historic Landmark, and is the Grand Canyon's most luxurious lodging. Refurbished in 1997, it boasts Oregon pine and native stone interiors that recall the old hunting lodges of Europe; it is the first example of rustic architecture in a national park. Today it has 78 rooms and suites, ranging from suites for $403 to standard rooms with a double bed for $163. All rooms are non-smoking, have cable television, air conditioning, telephone, and a full bath.

For information about ongoing art exhibits and activities in the hotel, or to check on same-night reservations, call Xanterra South Rim (928/638-2631). No pets.

Located just west of the El Tovar, the **Thunderbird** and **Kachina Lodges** were built in the 1960s to provide contemporary accommodations. The two-story identical structures are within easy walking distance of the canyon rim and Grand Canyon Village. Registration for the Thunderbird Lodge is at the Bright Angel Lodge, and registration for the Kachina Lodge is at the El Tovar Hotel. The Thunderbird and Kachina Lodges offer well-appointed rooms (all non-smoking) with canyon or park views, telephone, television, safe, in-room coffee, refrigerator, and a full bath. Prices range from $159 for a park-view room to $169 for a canyon-view room. Contact the Bright Angel Lodge or El Tovar Hotel for more information. No pets.

Built from the remains of historic Bright Angel Camp in 1935, the **Bright Angel Lodge** offers a choice of lodge rooms and rustic cabins along the canyon rim. Designed by architect Mary Colter, this log and native-stone structure has been called her crowning Grand Canyon achievement, with its environmentally sensitive, pioneer-style design and construction. A large wooden thunderbird, which she called "the Bright Angel of the sky," hangs above the mantle of the lobby's huge stone fireplace. Prices range from $73 for a basic room in the hiker's lodge to $163 for one of the special rim cabins (some have fireplaces). For about $314, you can stay in the historic Bucky O'Neill Cabin, the oldest continuously standing building on the rim, which has a fireplace, two televisions, a sitting room, and a bar. No pets.

For budget-minded visitors, the **Maswik Lodge,** located at the southwest end of Grand Canyon Village, offers modern lodge rooms and cabins, each with shower and telephone. Named for the Hopi *kachina* (spirit) who guards the Grand Canyon, the lodge is open year-round, with the cabins available May–October. Prices range from about $83 for a cabin to $159 for a room in the north wing of the lodge. No pets.

Nestled among the pinyon and juniper pygmy forests between Yavapai Point and the El Tovar Hotel is the park's largest lodging facility, **Yavapai Lodge.** It features year-round, modern motel-style accommodations in its east and west wings, while the main lodge provides registration, dining, and gift stores. The 358 units range in price from $99 in Yavapai West to $143 in Yavapai East. No pets.

North Rim

Designed by Gilbert Stanley Underwood (legendary architect of the Ahwahnee Hotel in Yosemite), the **Grand Canyon Lodge** (480/998-1981 or 877/386-4383) opened its doors to its first visitors in 1928. Designed as one of the great national park lodges, it's a National Historic Landmark featuring ponderosa pine and native stone throughout the main building. From the veranda and lounge areas, you can enjoy spectacular views of the canyon through enormous plate glass windows and expansive terraces. Its 174 cabins and 40 motel rooms are scattered near the main lodge building, in the ponderosa forest. Prices vary depending upon the type of guest accommodations, ranging $58–366.

Inner Canyon

Nestled beside Bright Angel Creek and a stand of cottonwood trees on the floor of the Inner Canyon, you'll find the Western-style cabins and main lodge of **Phantom Ranch**—an oasis that recalls the ranch hospitality of another era. Built in 1922, the Ranch is the only accommodation in the canyon and can only be reached by hiking, by mule, or by rafting the Colorado River. Prices vary depending on your mode of transportation. If you hike down, you can reserve a bed in one of the newer dorm buildings for $34.16. Hearty meals will run you $35.61 for a steak dinner, $22.60 for the hiker's stew, $10.14 for lunch, and $17.50 for breakfast. If you arrive on a mule, you'll pay about $401.16 for the first person or two for $709.46, with each additional person costing $321.11. There is also a two-night ride that runs $945.68 for parties of two, with prices varying depending upon the number of people. Because summer temperatures can reach 110°F on the canyon floor, the best time to visit Phantom Ranch is November–March. But beware, the secret's out about Phantom. You'll have to book a place here well in advance (up to 23 months) to get a chance to experience the Ranch and its unique wilderness setting.

If you bring your own room in the form of a recreational vehicle, you

can reserve space at Trailer Village year-round. There are 84 sites with picnic tables, barbeque grills, 30 and 50 amp electrical service, cable TV along
with water, and sewage hook-ups for hard-sided vehicles only. Showers and
laundry facilities are available nearby. Cost is $28 per space with a seven-
day limit.

Are there convenient places to stay just outside the park?

You can find lodging in several places near Grand Canyon National Park. Here are some options near the South and North Rims. Rates may vary depending on season.

SOUTH RIM

Tusayan (2 miles from the south entrance)

This collection of lodgings is closest to the park entrance.

Best Western Grand Canyon Squire Inn — $70–190
100 Hwy. 64 — 250 rooms, 4 suites
928/638-2681 or 800/622-6966
www.grandcanyonsquire.com
Southwestern decor resort hotel with Coronado Room Restaurant, coffee shop, pool, billiards, bowling, and video arcade.

Quality Inn and Suites — $60–210
Grand Canyon, Canyon Plaza — 76 rooms, 56 suites
Hwy. 64
928/638-2673 or 800/221-2222
www.grandcanyonqualityinn.com
A full service resort with buffet and restaurant, lounge, gift shop, seasonal outdoor pool, and indoor spa. All rooms have private balconies or patios.

Grand Hotel — $99–169
Hwy. 64 — 121 rooms
928/638-3333 or 888/634-7263
http://the-grand-hotel-grand-canyon.pacificahost.com
Grand Canyon's hotel with distinctive Southwestern decor, heated indoor pool, and Canyon Star Restaurant. Lobby has a fireplace, seating, Wi-Fi, and Starbucks station.

Holiday Inn Express Grand Canyon $74–335
Hwy. 64   164 rooms, 30 suites
928/638-3000 or 888/473-2269
www.grandcanyon.hiexpress.com
Award-winning Holiday Inn has merged with the Grand Canyon Suites to
offer, in addition to their Holiday rooms, stylish "Arizona Rooms," one- and
two-bedroom suites reminiscent of historic park lodges.

Red Feather Lodge Grand Canyon $60–150
Hwy. 64   231 rooms
928/638-2414 or 800/228-2000
www.redfeatherlodge.com
Canyon visitors with small pets welcome here! Heated pool, video game room,
and Cafe Tusayan restaurant.

Seven Mile Lodge (520/638-2291) is also located in Tusayan, but it does not
take reservations. You'll get a room at this small, affordable lodge ($75 single
or double) on a first-come, first-served basis.

Valle (27 miles from the south entrance)
Valle offers various visitor services including two gas stations, an amusement
park and campground, and a small airport with air museum.

Grand Canyon Inn $49–89
317 S. Hwy. 64   101 rooms
928/635-9203 or 800/635-9203
www.grand-canyon-inn.com
Seasonal pool, full service restaurant, and gift shop. No pets.

Williams (60 miles from the south entrance)
Williams, "Gateway to the Grand Canyon," is located in the heart of the beautiful Kaibab National Forest. It is at an elevation of 6,770 feet. You can stay
closer to the park, in Tusayan or Grand Canyon Village, but the closer you get,
the more you will pay. Check out www.thegrandcanyon.com for more details
about lodging and special events in this historic Southwestern town.

Canyon Country Inn B & B $54–89 (includes breakfast)
442 W. Route 66   13 rooms
928/635-2349 or 877/405-3280
www.thecanyoncountryinn.com
Charming teddy bear theme with delicious "beary" specials in the morning.
Private baths.

Canyon Motel & RV Park $50–136
1900 E. Rodeo Rd.   21 rooms in six cabooses/train cars
928/635-9371 or 800/482-3955
www.thecanyonmotel.com
Set in a lush pine forest, the charming rooms all have TVs; some have kitchenettes. Heated indoor pool. You can even spend the night in a retired train car!

Mountain Side Inn $63–103
642 E. Bill Williams Ave.   96 rooms
928/635-4431 or 800/462-9381
High country comforts overlooking 27 pine-filled acres. Heated pool and choice of hearty fare in Miss Kitty's Steakhouse and Saloon or the casual Dining Car Restaurant.

The Red Garter Bed & Bakery $120–145
137 W. Railroad Ave.   4 rooms
928/635-1484 or 800/328-1484
http://redgarter.com
Rave reviews from guests of this beautifully restored Victorian bordello and saloon. Listed in National Register of Historic Places. Comfortable rooms with names like "Best Gal's Room" and "Madam's Room," plus great breakfasts.

Sheridan House Inn $135–189 (includes breakfast)
460 E. Sheridan Ave.   7 rooms, 2 suites
888/635-9345
www.grandcanyonbbinn.com
Country charm in this art-filled house on two acres of pine forest. Evening social hour, bountiful breakfast buffet, outdoor spa. Lovely decks and a flagstone patio surround this distinctive inn.

Grand Canyon KOA (closed during winter) $47–52
5333 Hwy. 64
928/635-2307 or 800/KOA-5771
www.koa.com/where/az/03109
For those on wheels, this quiet off-highway campground offers indoor pool, convenience facilities, and 12 "Kamping Kabins" for rent. Reservations needed June–August.

Flagstaff (80 miles from the south entrance)

Although a bit farther from the park, you can find nice lodging in these facilities.

Aspen Inn B & B $99–139
218 North Elden St.   4 rooms
928/773-0295 or 888/999-4110
www.flagstaffbedbreakfast.com
In a restored 1912 home just a five-minute walk from downtown, this B & B offers a friendly mountain atmosphere. No minimum stays. Sorry no pets.

Best Western Pony Soldier $65–119 (includes continental breakfast)
3030 E. Route 66   90 rooms
928/526-2388 or 800/356-4143
www.bestwesternarizona.com
A life-size pony marks this two-story motel decorated in Southwestern motif. Heated indoor pool. Jalapeño Lou's Restaurant on premises.

Hilton Garden Inn $129–152
350 W. Forest Meadow St.   90 rooms
928/226-8888 or 800/333-0785
Heated indoor pool and exercise room. All rooms have TV and fridges.

InnSuites Hotel $59–113
1008 E. Route 66   130 rooms, 15 suites
928/774-7356 or 800/898-9124
http://flagstaff.innsuites.com
Complimentary hot breakfast buffet, evening beverage service, and free barbecue for guests on the first Wednesday of the month, all in a lovely pine forest setting.

Little America Hotel $129–250
2515 E. Butler Ave.   247 rooms
928/779-2741 or 800/865-1401
www.littleamerica.com
Luxurious rooms on 500 acres of ponderosa forest. Heated pool, dining room with a great brunch on Sundays, coffee shop, TV.

Radisson Woodlands Hotel
1175 W. Route 66
928/773-8888
www.flagstaffwoodlandshotel.com

$79–189
183 rooms, 17 suites

Elegance and comfort with heated pool and hot tub. Southwestern flavors in the Woodlands Cafe or entertaining Japanese teppan-style cooking in Sakura Restaurant and Sushi Bar.

NORTH RIM

Kaibab Lodge
Hwy. 67 (5 miles north of park entrance)
928/638-2389
www.kaibablodge.com

$95–155
30 rooms, 3 cabins

This lodge is open during the summer season only (mid-May–October). It includes a restaurant and campground.

Jacob Lake (32 miles north of park entrance)

Jacob Lake Inn
Intersection of Hwy. 89A and Hwy. 67
928/643-7232
www.jacoblake.com

$88–132
40 rooms

Built in 1932, this inn provides accommodations in cabins as well as hotel rooms nestled among the pines of Kaibab National Forest. It hosts a gift shop, lunch counter, dining room, and service station.

Where can we eat in the park?

G rand Canyon offers a full range of dining and snacking experiences, from historic dining rooms to casual cafeterias, fast-food joints, delis, and fountain shops. Kids get their own menus, the dress is always casual, and all eating areas are nonsmoking. Prices range from around $6 for breakfast at the Bright Angel Coffee Shop to almost $40 for a complete meal at the El Tovar Hotel. Many of the restaurants accept American Express, Visa, and MasterCard. If you want to make reservations or need more information, call Xanterra South Rim (928/638-2631).

South Rim

The fanciest evening meals on the South Rim of the Grand Canyon are served in the dining room at the **El Tovar Hotel.** The menu includes such fare as prime rib, steak, seafood, chicken, vegetarian, and daily specials, with prices that won't break the bank. Full-service breakfast (6:30–11 A.M.) and lunch (11:30 A.M.–2 P.M.) are also served along with dinner (5–10 P.M.) daily year-round. Advance reservations are advised, as guests without reservations often have a long wait. Dress is casual. Another good choice is the **Arizona Room,** located next to the Bright Angel Lodge on the rim. Here you'll enjoy dinner selections of wonderful broiled steaks, poultry, and seafood in a comfortable Western atmosphere. Dinner is served daily 4:30 P.M.–10 P.M., closed January and February. Lunch is served daily 11:30 P.M.–3 P.M., with no lunch service November–February.

Casual dining can be enjoyed at the **Bright Angel Restaurant** (in the Bright Angel Lodge, year-round daily 6:30 A.M.–10 P.M.), where dinner entrées include a wide selection of hearty meals, including vegetarian. Breakfast, lunch, and dinner are served daily. The lodge also hosts the **Canyon Coffee House** (varying hours, open seasonally) for a cup of shade-grown organic coffee, espresso, or cappuccino. Continental breakfast items are available. Stop by the nonsmoking **Bright Angel Bar** (near the top of Bright Angel Trail) for a drink and snack—ID is required. You may also hear Western singers or other musicians performing in the summer season.

If quick and easy eating is your goal, try one of the park's three cafeterias located at **Desert View Trading Post** (summer daily 8 A.M.–6 P.M., winter daily 9 A.M.–5 P.M.), **Maswik Lodge** (year-round daily 6 A.M.–10 P.M.), and the **Yavapai Lodge** (March–December breakfast daily 6–10:30 A.M., lunch and dinner daily 11 A.M.–9:30 P.M.). Self-service entrées and à la carte selections include salads, sandwiches, pasta, chicken, and pizza. All three cafeterias are open for breakfast, lunch, and dinner.

Fast-food options are found throughout the park. For quick snacks at one of the South Rim's most popular gathering places, check out the **Bright Angel Fountain** in the lodge right on the canyon rim. It offers hot dogs, sandwiches, ice cream, and cold drinks May–September daily 10 A.M.–8 P.M. Prices are reasonable, and all items are served to go. Or, try the **Delicatessen at the Marketplace** located in front of the General Store (year-round daily 8 A.M.–6 P.M., with additional seasonal hours). There you can get hot and cold sandwiches, chicken dinners, salads, and daily specials to eat there or to go. **Hermits Rest Snack Bar** (year-round daily 9 A.M.–5 P.M.), located next to Hermits Rest Gift Shop at the end of Hermit Road, offers quick snacks including hot dogs and light fare to go—access by shuttle only March–December or year-round by hiking. Lounges offering drinks and light snacks are located in most lodging facilities, including Bright Angel Lodge, Maswik Lodge, and the El Tovar Hotel.

North Rim

From May to October, you have several dining options on the North Rim, with prices to suit every budget. The fanciest meals can be enjoyed in the **Grand Canyon Lodge Dining Room** (928/638-2611), which serves continental meals with spectacular views of the canyon. Breakfast (6:30–10:30 A.M.), lunch (11:30 A.M.–2:30 P.M.), and dinner (4:45 P.M.–9:45 P.M.) are served daily. You can pick up quick snacks at inexpensive prices at the **Deli in the Pines** (daily 7 A.M.–9 P.M.). At the Lodge, there's also the **Rough Rider Saloon,** which has pastries and coffee in the morning (5:30–10:30 A.M.), and light fare, appetizers, and cocktails served around lunchtime and beyond (11:30 A.M.–11 P.M.). **The General Store** (located across from the North Rim Campground, daily 7 A.M.–8 P.M., but hours can vary with demand) has pizzas, snacks, and groceries at reasonable prices.

Inner Canyon

If you're lucky enough to get a reservation at Phantom Ranch, you'll be treated to some great home-style dining at the **Canteen.** A bountiful, family-style menu includes a hiker's stew, steak dinner, country breakfast, and sack lunch. You'll need to reserve in advance, with all meals served at prearranged times.

> ## What about dining in one of the nearby towns?

There are many good places to eat near Grand Canyon National Park. Here are just a few of them.

SOUTH RIM

Tusayan (2 miles from the south entrance):

You can find the usual assortment of fast-food places here plus restaurants in most of the hotels. If you have more time, you might want to try these establishments.

Canyon Star Restaurant and Saloon
Grand Hotel, Hwy. 64
928/638-3333
Delicious steaks, barbecue, Southwestern and Mexican food, live entertainment, and Western music. Breakfast, lunch, dinner, cocktails.

Coronado Room
Best Western Grand Canyon Squire Inn, 100 Hwy. 64
928/638-2681
The restaurant at this hotel has everything from escargot to elk steak with a large wine list. Casual dress.

The Saguaro Lounge
Best Western Grand Canyon Squire Inn, 100 Hwy. 64
928/638-2681
Sports bar with a family center (billiards, bowling, arcade games) offers light fare including pizza, nachos, Southwestern appetizers.

Williams (60 miles from the south entrance):

Here are a few food joints to check out in Williams.

Cruiser's Cafe 66
233 W. Route 66
928/635-2445
This shrine to the "Mother Road" is great for families. It features an old gas station setting, along with food such as calzones, steaks, ribs, and chicken. Lunch, dinner, cocktails.

Grand Canyon Coffee & Cafe
125 W. Route 66
928/635-4907
Grab your favorite coffee steamer or espresso, hot or frosted, plus bagels, sandwiches, salads. Breakfast, lunch, dinner.

Miss Kitty's Steakhouse & Saloon
642 E. Route 66
928/635-9161
Steaks, prime rib, barbecue chicken, plus live music on stage in the summer. Breakfast, dinner, cocktails.

Pancho McGillicuddy's
141 Railroad Ave.
928/635-4150
Williams's first Old West saloon sets the theme for fun at this Mexican cantina. Lunch, dinner, cocktails.

Pine Country Restaurant
107 N. Grand Canyon Blvd.
928/635-9718
Good home cooking, homemade pies a specialty. No adult beverages. Breakfast, lunch, dinner.

Rod's Steakhouse
301 E. Route 66
928/635-2671
Any restaurant in the same location for more than 50 years is doing something right! The name says it all—go for the beef. Lunch, dinner, cocktails. Closed Sundays.

Rosa's Cantina
106 S. 9th St.
928/635-0708
All spicy things Mexican, and great margaritas in the Double Deuce Cantina. Lunch, dinner, cocktails.

Flagstaff (80 miles from the south entrance):

Beaver Street Brewery and Whistle Stop Cafe
11 S. Beaver St.
928/779-0079
Wood-fired pizzas, specialty sandwiches, soup, salads, and fondue. Lunch, dinner, cocktails.

Black Bart's Steakhouse & Musical Revue
2760 E. Butler Ave.
800/574-4718
Nightly musical revue with your steak, chicken, seafood, or ribs. Dinner, cocktails.

Brandy's Restaurant and Bakery
1500 E. Cedar Ave. #40
928/779-2187
The bagels at this favorite Flagstaff, Arizona restaurant are the only hand-formed, boiled, and baked bagels in town. All of the Danish pastries, cookies, scones, bread puddings, brownies, muffins, etc., are hand crafted daily. Breakfast, lunch, dinner.

Chez Marc Bistro
503 N. Humphreys St.
928/774-1343
Country French dining in historic
house. Lunch, dinner, cocktails.

Cottage Place Restaurant
126 W. Cottage Ave.
928/774-8431
Fine dining in restored 1909 bungalow. Beer and wine only. Dinner. Closed Mondays.

La Bellavia
18 S. Beaver St.
928/774-8301
Located in the historic Merle Saver building, serving pancakes, sandwiches, soups, and salads. Breakfast, lunch.

Mama Luisa
2710 N. Steves Blvd.
928/526-6809
Delicious Italian fare in casual, cozy setting. Dinner, cocktails.

Mason Jar Restaurant
2610 E. Route 66
928/526-9474
Cobblers and home-style cookin'—
as American as Route 66. Breakfast,
lunch, dinner, cocktails.

San Felipe's Cantina
103 N. Leroux St.
928/779-6000
Coastal Mexican food and cocktails.

NORTH RIM

Kaibab Lodge Dining Room
Highway 67 (5 miles north of park entrance)
928/638-2389
Serves good and hearty meals. Breakfast, lunch, dinner. May 15–October 15 only.

Jacob Lake Inn Coffee Shop & Dining Room
(32 miles north of park entrance)
Intersection of Highways 89A & 67
928/643-7232
Home-cooked hearty American fare with local specialties including baked
trout and fresh baked goods. Reasonable prices—an entire meal will run you
$5.95. Breakfast, lunch, dinner. Open year-round.

With nearly 25 established picnic areas situated near some of the park's most scenic lookouts on both the South and North Rims, the Grand Canyon is the ultimate picnic spot. Where you finally decide to spread your tablecloth is up to you, but here are some choices for stocking up on goods.

If you don't want to do the legwork, you can pick up a box lunch from the cafeteria at Maswik Lodge or the Canyon Café at Yavapai Lodge. Box lunches generally include a choice of sandwich, a piece of fruit, a drink, peanuts, chips, and a cookie.

For sandwiches and drinks made to order and to go, you have lots of options, including the delicatessens at the three DNPS General Stores. These stores are located near the visitor center in Grand Canyon Village, at Desert View, and in Tusayan. Or, if you want to put together your own picnic supplies, cruise the grocery aisles of these stores.

Are there any special seasonal events in the Grand Canyon?

You bet. During the first three weeks of September, the park hosts the Grand Canyon Music Festival (P.O. Box 1332, Grand Canyon, AZ 86023, 928/638-9215 or 800/997-8285, www.grandcanyonmusicfest.org) at the Shrine of Ages auditorium, next to the visitor center on the South Rim at 7:30 P.M. Co-sponsored by the National Park Service, the festival brings musicians from across the country to perform sold-out concerts to audiences of residents and visitors alike. Tickets cost $15 for adults and $8 for children (no children under six, please) and can be purchased in advance by phone. You can also purchase tickets at the door, unless the performance is sold out.

Throughout the year, the El Tovar Hotel hosts events including art exhibits, Native American craft markets, and music performances for the enjoyment of park visitors. Call Xanterra South Rim (928/638-2631) for more information and a schedule of activities.

During the winter, Grand Canyon celebrates the holidays with Christmas festivities and cheer, including a 20-foot-tall Christmas tree in the lobby of the El Tovar and a Christmas Eve and Christmas night celebration at Phantom Ranch, hosted by the ranch hands.

V
Camping
and
Backpacking

It wouldn't be one of our great national parks without a slew of camping choices. Let's run down the options in each area, from pitching a tent to hooking up your fully equipped RV. Of course, camping prices are subject to change.

SOUTH RIM

Camping on the South Rim is generally restricted to established campgrounds, although a few remote sites are available with a backcountry permit. Coin-operated laundry and showers are available near Mather Campground. A sanitary dump station is located near Mather and Trailer Village and is open mid-May–mid-October.

Mather Campground

Mather, a year-round campsite located near the visitor center in Grand Canyon Village, is a large campground run by the NPS (877/444-6777, www.recreation.gov). There are 326 individual tent and RV sites (no hookups available, 30-foot trailer or RV maximum), and reservations are strongly recommended March 1–mid-November. Reservations can be made up to six months in advance, with sites costing $18 (up to six people, three tents and two vehicles) to $50 (group site with a maximum of 50 people and three vehicles per site). The rest of the year, Mather operates on a first-come, first-served basis, at a price of $15–30 per site. Leashed pets are allowed and may not be left unattended in your tent, RV, or car. Coin-operated laundry and showers are located nearby.

Trailer Village

Trailer Village, open year-round, is adjacent to Mather Campground, just 0.5 mile from the canyon rim. It offers 80 RV sites with 30 and 50 amp electrical service, cable TV, water, sewage, picnic table, and grill at a cost of $28 per site for two people, and $2 for each additional person. Reservations are recommended and can be made through Xanterra Parks (888/297-2757, www.grandcanyonlodges.com); for same-day reservations call Xanterra South Rim (928/638-2631). Leashed pets are allowed and may not be left unattended in your RV. Coin-operated showers, telephones, vending machines, and laundry are nearby.

Desert View Campground

Desert View Campground, with 50 sites for tents and small RVs, is open mid-May–mid-October and is located near the east entrance, 26 miles east of Grand Canyon Village. There are no hookups and no reservations, just first-come, first-served, at a cost of about $12 per site (water and toilets available). Leashed pets are allowed and may not be left unattended in your tent, RV, or car.

NORTH RIM

Camping on the North Rim is only possible mid-May–mid-October, weather permitting. Before or after these times, you're dealing with some serious weather. Come to think of it, you might get some nasty weather even when it's open. It's generally a rougher experience, with fewer facilities and visitor services.

North Rim Campground

North Rim Campground is operated by the NPS (877/444-6777, www.recreation.gov) and located a mile from the rim. There are 84 individual tent and RV sites (no hookups, but there is a dump site) at a price of $18–25 per site. Reservations are strongly recommended and can be made up to six months in advance. Coin-operated showers are located nearby, open 7 A.M.–9 P.M. Water, restrooms, and group sites are also available. Leashed pets are allowed and may not be left unattended in your tent, RV, or car.

INNER CANYON

There are only three developed campgrounds in the Inner Canyon, all of which are located along the corridor trails. They are Indian Garden Campground below the South Rim; Bright Angel Campground near Phantom Ranch; and Cottonwood Campground below the North Rim. All three require backcountry permits. These sites come without water, toilets, emergency phones, or similar amenities.

> What are the campgrounds outside the park?

If you can't get a spot at one of the campgrounds inside the park, you can always try your luck at one of the sites outside park boundaries. We'll list your options according to area.

South Rim

The U.S. Forest Service operates a public campground (no hookups or dump station) at **Ten-X Campground,** located two miles south of Tusayan and 4.3 miles from the entrance of the Park. It's open mid-April–September. Try to get there early, as its 70 sites tend to fill up fast in this ponderosa pine forest campground. There is a self-guided nature trail and occasional weekend evening campfire programs at the amphitheater. Cost is $10 per site, with picnic tables, fire rings, barbecue grills, water, and pit toilets. No showers or reservations. Group sites are available at $75–200 for up to 150 people, but you must have a reservation (928/638-2443, www.fs.fed.us/r3/kai/recreation/campgrounds/TenX.shtml).

You may also find a good place to camp in the national forest outside the park. Restrictions may apply for "at large" camping; for example, camping is not allowed within a quarter-mile of Highway 64. For more information, call 928/638-2443, or write the Tusayan Ranger District (Kaibab National Forest, P.O. Box 3088, Grand Canyon, AZ 86023).

You RV cowboys may find a place to park at **Camper Village** (928/638-2887, grand@grandcanyonactivities.com), a privately run operation open April–October with 200 sites on 10 acres. It is located seven miles south of Grand Canyon Village in Tusayan. Fees range from about $22 per day for a tent and $27 for a teepee that sleeps five, to $50 for trailer space with water, electric, and sewer. Leashed pets are welcome. There's also a general store, ATM, food service, coin-operated showers, and petting zoo.

North Rim

Like everything at the North Rim, camping outside the park here is seasonal and depends greatly on the weather. Open mid-May–mid-October, **DeMotte Campground** (928/643-7395), run by the U.S. Forest Service, is located seven miles north of the entrance to the Grand Canyon National Park's North Rim. The 38 single-unit sites are available on a first-come, first-served basis only and offer water, pit toilets, grills, and picnic tables for $16 a night for one vehicle and $8 for a second vehicle for up to six people (no hookups or dump station).

Jacob Lake Campground (928/643-7395), also located on national forest property, is 32 miles north of the entrance station. There are 53 sites available on a first-come, first-served basis mid-May–November 1, depending on snow-fall. Cost is $12 a night for one vehicle and $6 for a second vehicle for up to six people (no hookups or dump station)—group sites are available. Note that this campground will be closed for the 2008 season.

Open May 15–October 15 only, **Kaibab Camper Village** (summer 928/643-7804 or winter 928/526-0924, www.kaibabcampervillage.com) is privately run and is located a quarter-mile south of Jacob Lake on Highway 67. There are 60 RV spaces and 20 tent sites. Tents sites are $17 a night, and sites with hookups are $33 per night. Hookups, fire pits, picnic tables, toilets, coin-operated showers, coin-operated laundry, and outside sinks are available, and reservations are accepted. Pets are welcome.

Dispersed camping is permitted in the national forest outside the park. This means no facilities, no water, and many regulations. To find out what they are, contact the Kaibab National Forest (800 S. 6th St., Williams, AZ 86046, 928/635-8200, www.fs.fed.us/r3/kai).

Are there limits or restrictions on camping at Grand Canyon?

You probably guessed the answer—yes, there are rules and restrictions. But it's all for a good cause, mainly to protect both you and the canyon from unnecessary harm. Camping outside designated areas is prohibited and strictly monitored, and rule breakers may receive a hefty fine.

We hope our campers follow the golden rule of camping: Leave No Trace. That means packing out all your trash, staying on main trails and not short-cutting switchbacks, keeping your fires in the grills, and not gathering wood. Wood and charcoal may be purchased at the general store. Remember, no open fires.

Squirrels, coyotes, and other campground scavengers are always on the prowl for goodies. Store food and any fragrant items (such as shampoo, tooth-paste, and soap) safely out of reach, either in your car or in a backpack. You'll need to hang your backpacks from a tree or rack to keep the critters out.

Backcountry campers need to obtain a permit. They also need to follow a special set of rules to keep our wilderness areas as pristine as possible. Keep loud voices and noises down, pack out trash, and use camp stoves instead of fires. You'll need to bury human waste at least 200 feet from trails, campsites, and water sources. (Bury waste in a hole 4–6 inches deep and in diameter.) Pack out toilet paper in plastic bags rather than burning or burying it. Many wildfires have been started by burning trash and toilet paper. Any washing (of clothes, bodies, dishes, etc.) should be done at least 200 feet from water sources, and scatter strained dishwater.

Can we build a campfire?

A campfire's comforting crackle is one of the best parts of camping, but it has caused some of our forest fires. As long as you follow a few guidelines, our next generation of campers will be able to enjoy fireside gatherings as well.

Fires are prohibited below the rims due to wood shortages and wildfire dangers. It's probably for the best; fire remains can be a real eyesore, and that charcoal and ash can take hundreds of years to break down in this arid climate. Also, collecting wood is not allowed anywhere in the park. Break that rule, and you might collect a fine from a ranger. You can only build fires in the campgrounds where grills are provided. Ground fires and the building of fire rings are prohibited.

Now, some safety measures. Start by using those established fire pits, then check around the area for potential spark hazards. Never leave fires unattended; put them out by stirring in water before you leave the campground, and do a final check for any remaining embers. For the sake of protecting our wilderness environment, backpackers are asked to use small portable stoves for cooking and boiling water.

What special activities can we find around the campgrounds?

Campers often want to learn more about this awesome place called the Grand Canyon. That's where the ranger programs come in. Take a look at *The Guide* or drop by a visitor center to find out more about all the available activities. Here's a sampling of programs that have been offered in the past by the park staff. (Note that the programs are subject to cancellation due to rain, snow, or lightning and may not be offered year-round.)

One way to take in the wonder of the place while learning more about it is to join a ranger-led hike. The strenuous three-mile Cedar Ridge Hike takes about 3–4 hours and goes 1,140 feet down the unpaved South Kaibab Trail to Cedar Ridge. If you want to learn about the culture of the canyon, you can join a ranger for The Human Story get-together on the back porch of the El Tovar Hotel. Geology at the Canyon: Read the Rocks is an easy one-mile hike on paved roads that meets at the Yavapai Observation Station. This walk explores the geologic events that created the Grand Canyon, taking you back 250 million years to a time when sea creatures lived in the area.

Evening programs allow you to see the starlit side of the canyon. Nightly activities meet at the Mather Amphitheater, located behind the Park Headquarters of the Rim Trail (during the winter, they meet inside the Shrine of Ages next to the center). Allow an hour for the slideshow, dress warmly, and bring a flashlight.

In the Desert View area, there are a few programs designed to enhance your knowledge of the canyon's history and wildlife. Glimpses of the Past, which meets at the Tusayan Museum, focuses on the ancient people who called the canyon home 800 years ago. One hour before sunset, join The Spirit of Sunset program to watch the sun sink in the west and hear a ranger talk—dress warmly.

Where can we rent camping gear and buy supplies inside the park?

No matter how prepared you think you are for a camping excursion in the Grand Canyon, there's a chance some vital piece of equipment slipped through the cracks. ("Honey, you forgot the tent and sleeping bags.")

If you find yourself in the park, ready to camp but completely unprepared, head to the General Store at Market Plaza in Grand Canyon Village or the General Store in the North Rim Campground. You can buy or rent tents, sleeping bags, sleeping pads, stoves, and fuel at Market Plaza. No rentals are available at the North Rim Campground. They also have groceries, film, and other basic items. The nearest place outside the park to find the full range of items is probably Flagstaff, Arizona, about 1.5–2 hours away.

Wherever you get your camping gear, make sure you have a tent with rainfly, ground cloth, warm sleeping bag, sleeping pad, flashlight, extra socks, food, cooking stove and fuel, pot, spoon, cup, water bottle, and any personal gear.

Are there any organized trips into the backcountry?

There are so many, it will make your head spin. We're no longer dealing with simple options like, "Should I ride a mule or walk?" Today you have a multitude of choices; in fact, there are so many that I can't mention them all here. What I can do is to give you a taste of some interesting stuff the backcountry outfitters are up to these days.

The Grand Canyon Field Institute (P.O. Box 399, Grand Canyon, AZ 86023, 928/638-2485 or 866/471-4435, www.grandcanyon.org/fieldinstitute) is the field seminar program for the Grand Canyon Association, co-sponsored by the National Park Service. Classes explore the natural and cultural history of the Grand Canyon with day hikes, backpacking, yoga classes, and more. During the spring and summer, you can take three-day introductory backpacking trips for about $535. In October the GCFI offers five-day geology exploration trips from rim to rim for about $660. There are natural history hikes, photography excursions, hikes just for women, birding treks, Native American history hikes, and many other options. Contact the GCFI for a complete listing of trips.

And that's just one of the organizations that offers trips! Around the Grand Canyon, you have lots of other adventure providers just waiting to dazzle the spirit with mountain bike trips, river excursions, horseback trips, and much more.

When and why do we need a backcountry permit?

A pessimist might say that backcountry permits (which cost about $10, plus $5 per person, per night camped below the rim and $5 per group per night camped above the rim, prices subject to change) are just another way for the NPS to make a profit. But permits serve a very important function: They allow rangers to protect both you and the park from overuse. Also, about 400 hikers (mostly day hikers) per year need rescue assistance in the Grand Canyon. Believe me, those rescued hikers would be happy to pay for another permit.

A backcountry permit is required for all overnight use of the backcountry, including hiking, horseback-riding, cross-country ski trips, off-river hikes by river-trip members, overnight camping on the North Rim during the winter, and camping at rim sites other than developed campgrounds. Permits for all overnight use must be obtained through the Backcountry Information Center. And, once your itinerary is established, you are required to follow the exact plan authorized on the permit.

Every year, the requests for permits (30,000 for backcountry permits) far outweigh the allowed use limits (13,000 permits), which were established to protect the canyon and the quality of visitors' experience. For this reason, advance reservations are strongly recommended, and they can be made up to four months in advance. While the permit allows you access to the backcountry, it does not reserve a specific tent site within the backcountry.

There are three ways to apply for a permit:

- Bring your request in person to the Backcountry Information Center (preferred method).

- Fax your request to the Backcountry Information Center at 928/638-2125.

- Mail your request to the Backcountry Information Center, Grand Canyon National Park, P.O. Box 129, Grand Canyon, AZ 86023.

When sending in a permit request, the preferred method of payment is with a credit card. Be sure to indicate the maximum amount you authorize the Backcountry Information Center to charge so that your longest trip alternative can be considered. Valid personal checks and money orders against a United States bank are also accepted when made out for the correct amount. For more information, contact the Backcountry Office (928/638-7875, phone hours Mon.–Fri. 1–5 P.M. MST, except federal holidays, www.nps.gov/grca/planyourvisit/backcountry-permit.htm). At the website, you can also download a PDF of the permit application.

When is the best time of year to visit the Grand Canyon's backcountry?

I'd like to say anytime is the right time, but the Grand Canyon is a land of extremes, from the banks of the Colorado River to the high desert. My favorite time is in October—fewer crowds on the rim, but among the busiest backcountry-use months, with normally moderate temperatures. Summer is very hot and very crowded, but sometimes that's the only time people can get away. Winter can be downright nasty, with icy and snowy conditions. The best time of year to explore the backcountry depends on what you want and are able to do. But all things being equal, your safest bets are the late spring and early fall. Here are some special considerations for those of you thinking about other times of the year.

South Rim

The South Rim is located on an exposed high desert with wildly fluctuating temperatures. When exploring the backcountry here in the summer, remember to be prepared for intense sun and drenching thunderstorms. Winter temperatures average about 30°F, well within the range of a nasty winter. Bring all the essentials to stay warm and dry.

North Rim

During the winter, approximately late October–mid-May, the only access to the North Rim is by hiking, snowshoeing, or cross-country skiing. As long as you can endure the conditions (up to 150 inches of snow per year), you'll be rewarded with an uncrowded, pristine look at the canyon.

Inner Canyon

Summer in the Inner Canyon is literally like playing with fire. We're talking temperatures well above 100°F, and it doesn't take long to suffer the effects of that kind of heat. Winter conditions in the canyon are generally a little milder than on the rims (average 58°F). But that's not to say you won't get an ice storm or snowstorm once you venture below the rim. For that reason, our pack mules are fitted with special ice shoes, and we recommend the same thing for you hikers. You can rent or buy crampons for your boots at the General Store in Grand Canyon Village.

What is the Grand Canyon's backcountry like?

Like nothing you've ever seen. However spectacular you've imagined the Grand Canyon to be, the real thing will take your breath away.

The surrounding plateau lands—stark, wild, and elegant—are adorned with sagebrush and grasses that give the desert its distinct aroma, especially after a rain. Closer to the canyon rims, desert scrub mixes with pinyon-juniper woodlands and stands of ponderosa pines. On the North Rim are boreal forests of spruce, fir, and aspen. The canyon itself remains practically hidden until you reach the edge and come face-to-face with its booming expanse of sheer cliffs and chiseled stratification.

The descent into the canyon is a journey into an even hotter, drier world. While the temperature at the top might be 75°F, once you reach the bottom you may be seeking shade in 105-degree weather. In this severe environment, plants adapt their shape and color to take advantage of what little moisture there is. You'll see hearty shrubs with small leaves and short stems, as if puckered against the dry, red soil. Some leaves are covered with a waxy material to seal in moisture, while others are covered with tiny gray hairs that deflect sunlight and grab moisture. Root systems are shallow, sometimes reaching into the rock crevices to brace against the wind and run-off.

Canyon animals migrate, hibernate, and endure all the seasonal changes. You may see mammals and birds traveling between the rims in search of a suitable and comfortable environment. The hottest regions host creatures that wander the nighttime hours and simply find a hole to crawl in during the day.

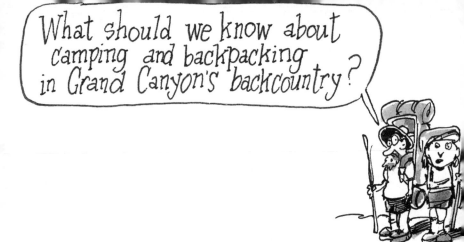

What should we know about camping and backpacking in Grand Canyon's backcountry?

A wilderness excursion is a bit different than a stroll through Grand Canyon Village. You should check with the nearest ranger station or visitor center for current weather and trail conditions before you embark—and then be prepared for the possibility that the forecast is completely wrong. Hiking the backcountry requires an ample amount of time for resting and setting up your campsite. The park has some suggestions and regulations that will help you enjoy your trip while preserving Grand Canyon's fragile backcountry areas.

There are 16 main trails and many small routes in the Inner Canyon, but only the corridor trails (Bright Angel and Kaibab) are maintained and checked regularly by trail crews. Remember, none of these trails is easy, not when you're dealing with such extreme elevation changes and weather conditions. Plan carefully—bring enough food and water, proper clothing, and a map and compass—and know your physical limitations. The sweltering heat has been known to disorient people and lead them to actions they might not otherwise attempt.

You must get a permit to camp anywhere in the park other than developed campgrounds on the rims. The only exception to the rule is for those staying at Phantom Ranch (but they still need to make accommodation reservations).

Backcountry permits are currently $10, plus $5 per person per night (subject to change), and can be obtained up to four months in advance through the Backcountry Information Center. If you arrive without a permit and wish to get one, you can put your name on a waiting list by showing up at the Backcountry Information Center at 8 A.M. on the day you wish to hike. Your chances of getting a same-day permit is unlikely; you should plan for a 1–3 day (or longer) wait. The South Rim Backcountry Information Center is open daily for walk-in visitors 8 A.M.–noon and 1–5 P.M. MST. The North Rim Backcountry Information Center is open mid-May–mid-October for walk-in visitors 8 A.M.–noon and 1–5 P.M. MST. Advance reservations are highly recommended. To help you plan your visit, know that the busiest times to hike the canyon are spring, fall, and any school vacation period.

Once you get your permit and are ready to embark, remember a few helpful tips. Try to schedule at least two nights in the canyon, so that you have a chance to rest before you hike back out. For rim-to-rim hikes, a minimum of three nights is suggested.

Hikes from the South Rim begin at 7,000 feet above sea level. You can depart from the South Rim any time of year (though you may need crampons in winter). The North Rim begins at 8,500 feet. This high altitude can cause all sorts of symptoms, like fatigue, dizziness, nausea, and headache. So take it slow at first. North Rim hiking trips can be taken mid-May–late October.

Many species of desert plants concentrate poisonous material from the soil in their stems and leaves. The canyon is not a good place to experiment with eating wild foods.

Do your washing and cleaning at least 200 feet from the water source (not in it!). Purify all water taken from natural sources by using iodine or bleach or by boiling or filtering. Use toilets where provided, and bury feces at least 200 feet from trails, campsites, and water sources.

Wood or ground fires are not allowed beneath the rims. Backpacking stoves are allowed at all campsites.

And please remember, the greatest good you can do for the canyon is to leave no trace that you were ever here. Translation: Pack out all your trash.

Flash floods can appear literally out of the blue. Skies are clear, the sun is shining, yet some distant rainstorm might be sending a wall of water down the canyon, taking everything in its path. Hikers have been killed in flash floods generated from thunderstorms as far as 25 miles away. There is no overstating the dangers of flash flooding in a natural corridor like the Grand Canyon.

Take what precautions you can, like:

- Before you head out study maps of your hike plan to identify possible escape routes.

- Be especially careful in the slot canyons of Grand, Marble, and Glen Canyon regions—they can be extremely dangerous when it rains. Be particularly alert in areas that are prone to flooding like streambeds, washes, narrow canyon, and spots that are specifically posted with flash flood warning signs.

- Never camp in dry washes when there is even the remotest possibility of flooding (which is pretty much always). If you must camp in a wash, be sure to camp as high as possible.

- Always face upstream when near or in any creek or drainage. Do not cross flowing water or flooded trails when the water is above your knees.

- If you see or hear a flood coming move to higher ground immediately—do not try to outrun a flood. Warn other people downstream if a flash flood occurs.

NOT A GOOD IDEA

WHERE IS TUWEEP?

Read it and weep: Tuweep is a remote, rugged section of wilderness near the entrance to the park's North Rim. Mohave County Road 5, a few miles west of Fredonia, is the only entrance road, and its 60 miles of graded dirt may become impassable during wet weather. There are no visitor services at Tuweep—no water, food, lodging, fuel, or transportation. Fredonia, Arizona, 69 miles away, is the nearest town.

Sound like a friendly place to visit, or what? Actually, for those adventuresome enough to make the journey out here, there is a wealth of natural beauty to discover. At its elevation of 5,500 feet, Tuweep has open spaces, grasslands, sage, and pinyon-juniper woodland. Its striking canyon vistas reveal the history of its volcanic origins, with rounded cinder cones rising from the valley floor, remnants of ancient lava flows welded to the canyon walls, and the astonishing sight of the Colorado River flowing 3,000 feet below.

The NPS operates a free campground that is open year-round. The 10 sites, available on a first-come, first-served basis, have composting toilets, picnic tables and fire grates but no water. There is one additional group site that may be reserved by calling 928/638-7870. You may find the campground rather crowded on Memorial Day and other spring and summer weekends, but beyond that, you may have the place to yourself.

Points of interest include the Tuweep Ranger Station (928/716-2843), which is on the National Register of Historic Places. The area offers a few great hiking trails, like Tuckup, Saddle Horse Canyon, and Lava Falls. Permits for overnight hiking are required.

WHERE ISSSS TUWEEEP?!!

Will we have any problems with animals in the wilderness?

As you may have learned already in this book, the most notorious troublemakers among Grand Canyon's wildlife are squirrels and chipmunks. This holds true in the backcountry, where the little critters must have picked up a trick or two from their relatives in Grand Canyon Village.

Every year, Arizona reports cases of the bubonic plague (yes, THE plague), which can be carried by squirrels and their fleas. Canyon squirrels, which can carry rabies, are beggars who bite, so avoid the temptation to strike up a food exchange program when they visit your campsite. That way, you can avoid infection and a trip to the clinic for some painful shots. Other aggressive critters you may encounter include deer mice and ravens. To keep the animals AND your food safe, you should take care to store your food carefully:

- Use an animal-proof food storage container such as a Rat Sack—a lightweight wire mesh bag that you can rent or purchase at the Canyon Village Marketplace on the South Rim, through the Backcountry Information Center, or at other outlets. Metal ammunition cases are provided at every campsite at Indian Garden, Bright Angel, and Cottonwood Campgrounds—use them!

- Never leave food, even in your pack, unattended.

- Carefully inspect your cooking/eating area. Clean up any food crumbs or other trash so you do not entice scavengers.

DANGER

BEGGARS CAN BE BITERS!

• Anything aromatic—powder, ointment, toothpaste, sunscreen, lotions, utensils—must be stored with your food in your animal-proof container. Animals are not selective; they are drawn by any enticing smell.

• Leave nothing inside your pack overnight, and leave all pockets and compartments unzipped. This allows nocturnal visitors to snoop around without tempting them to gnaw at your gear out of curiosity.

- Hanging food may still be accessible to ringtails, mice, and ravens. Hanging food can also damage trees, a valuable shade resource in the desert—use an animal-proof storage container instead.

- Pack out all your trash, including left-over food.

- NEVER FEED WILDLIFE.

Other animals to consider are snakes and scorpions. Rattlesnakes do live in the canyon; however, they are naturally shy animals that will bite only if surprised or extremely provoked. To avoid catching one off-guard, make some noise (screaming isn't necessary, just some foot-shuffling or whistling) when you're walking on the trail. Scorpions are easily avoided by shaking out your shoes in the morning. They like dark, warm places (we won't talk about the smell), so before you slip on those sneakers, take a second and knock them around a bit.

VI

Recreational Opportunities

The Grand Canyon, the Colorado River, and the surrounding lands offer many opportunities for all types of recreation. The only wild card is the climate—hot and arid in the summer, freezing and snowy in the winter. For those who are ready for extreme weather, the area is a mecca for outdoor activities.

Walking

A leisurely walk along either the South or North Rim, with stops at museums, visitor centers, ancestral Anasazi sites, and historic structures, can be a perfect introduction to the park. There are 10 miles of maintained walking trails along the South Rim, and more than 20 miles of maintained trails along the North Rim.

Hiking

A journey on our 588 miles of rim and canyon trails (including 51 miles of maintained trails) begins with a single step. From strolls through a ponderosa pine forest along the rim, to steep descents into the canyon, our many paths take you through the Grand Canyon's most spectacular landscapes and back-country areas. For those who want to stay close to the main visitor areas in the park, try a short jaunt on a trail below the rims.

Bicycling

For a swifter but more challenging tour, you can bike on all paved and secondary roadways along the rims April–October. No two-wheelers are allowed on any rim or canyon trails except for the new Greenway Trail. There are some fun gravel roads for good mountain biking in national forest lands surrounding the park. It's best if you bring your own bike, since rentals are not available in the park, and the closest shops are located in Flagstaff or Sedona, Arizona.

River Rafting and Running

Year-round, the Grand Canyon vicinity provides awesome river recreation.

A one-day, smooth-water float trip along the Colorado runs April–October, while oar- or motor-powered white-water rafting trips that run 3–18 days lure experienced river runners and visitors year-round. Be prepared for cold water temperatures and some of the world's swiftest currents. All river trips are guided by experienced and licensed outfitters.

Fishing

Some of the best fishing in the park happens at either end of the canyon. At the western end, there's great fishing along 16 miles of the Colorado River from Lees Ferry to Lake Mead. At the western tip, Lake Mead offers good fishing and other water recreation opportunities. If you're up for a hike or mule ride, you can try your luck around Phantom Ranch, about nine miles below the South Rim. An Arizona State Fishing License is required.

Swimming

Although swimming seems like a natural activity in a place with such a big river running through it, do not try to swim in the mighty Colorado. Powerful currents and temperatures of 45–50°F have taken many lives. You'll have better luck in some of the side streams, although cold temperatures still pose hypothermia risks. For these reasons, we generally don't encourage swimming as a recreational activity. You also won't find any swimming pools in the park.

Horseback Riding

Mule rides in the Grand Canyon have been popular since the 1890s. Riding a horse or mule into the canyon or in the surrounding forests is great fun, and there are several ways to do it, on your own or with a licensed outfitter. For milder excursions, take a one- or two-hour horseback trail ride with a wrangler/guide. These rides begin at the corrals at Apache Stables in Tusayan, just outside the park's south entrance, and take you through national forest lands on the South Rim.

Cross-Country Skiing and Snowshoeing

Some of the park's best-kept secrets are winter activities. There's cross-country skiing through South Rim national forests and, although the North Rim area is closed following the first snow, you can try your luck skiing or snowshoeing into the park on Jacob Lake Road.

How much of the park is accessible to hikers?

The entire park is accessible to hikers, but unless you have the survival instincts of a chuckwalla, you have to be an expert with a map and compass to travel off-trail. When you hike the trails in the park, you're carrying on a tradition that goes back thousands of years. These trails— trekked by Native Americans, pioneers, and generations of backpackers and hikers—are your best shot at getting an insider's look at the Grand Canyon.

Most of the park's 1.2 million acres extend across dry, rugged backcountry with plenty of scenic wonders for the curious hiker. To enjoy your experience, you'll need to take responsibility for your own safety and for preserving this dynamic and fragile national park.

Here are a few hints for getting the most out of your hiking adventure:

- Begin your hike by stopping by a ranger station or visitor center for information on current trail conditions. Trails can be temporarily closed due to unexpected weather. It's best to be an informed hiker, not a disappointed one.

- Allow plenty of time for your hiking adventure: Plan for at least twice as much time to hike out as to hike in. Don't forget that the Grand Canyon is a mountain that you'll have to hike back up, after your long hike down. Remember, uphill hikers have the right of way!

- The terrain below the rims is a desert. Always plan to carry and drink at least 0.5–1 quart of water or sports drink for every hour hiking in the canyon, and eat high-energy snacks or salty foods often to keep up your stamina on hikes lasting longer than 30 minutes. Plan your hike so you don't travel long distances without allowing adequate time to rest, cool down, and enjoy the spectacular scenery. When hiking in the demanding terrain of the Grand Canyon, you need to eat about twice as much as you do normally.

- Except for short day hikes, always try to hike with a companion. Inform others of your plans, and stick to them so you can be found in case of emergency.

- Wear layered clothing, as temperatures rise during a descent into the canyon. A waterproof cover-up will help when the weather suddenly changes. Take along some moleskin in case of blisters, sunscreen, sunglasses, and a hat.

- Travel lightly. The heaviest items in your pack should be food and water, but don't skimp on the essentials such as a map, compass, signal mirror or whistle, first aid kit, and water purification tablets.

- When encountering mules on the trail, remember that our four-legged friends and their passengers have the right of way. Be sure to follow any instructions from wranglers, step off of the trail on the uphill side away from the edge, and wait for the animals to get at least 50 feet past you before returning to the trail.

- Help keep our backcountry areas clean for everyone by packing out all your trash and garbage.

What should we take on our day hike?

WATER!! WATER!!

In a word, **WATER.** For any kind of walk or hike in the Grand Canyon, water is your best friend. Day hikes are fairly easy to prepare for, but backpacking trips are a whole different matter. A jaunt into the backcountry for several days will probably mean investing in some equipment and clothes.

Here's a rundown on summer day-hiking essentials. Don't pack too much, as you never want to take more than you can easily carry—especially in the heat. Start with a pair of sturdy, comfortable sneakers, lightweight hiking boots, or hiking shoes with good traction—and be sure that they are broken in. Hiking boots are recommended for Hermit, Grandview, and other unmaintained trails. During hot summer days, a hat that keeps the sun off your head and a shirt that protects your upper body will help you maintain a safe body temperature. If you become overheated, you can cool down by pouring water on your hat and shirt. Shorts and cotton T-shirts are popular for hiking, but if the weather changes, you'll be glad to have a pair of loose pants and a shirt made of material that dries quickly, like nylon, capilene, or a nylon/cotton blend; these types of clothing also layer nicely. During our cooler months and even late on a summer day, a water- and wind-proof shell with attached hood is essential in case of a sudden downpour.

A small, comfortable daypack, knapsack, or fanny pack to carry plenty of water is essential. Make sure you carry 0.5–1 quart of water per hour per person (more on hot days or strenuous hikes)—and make sure you drink it! Take along nutritious, high-energy snacks that you can munch along the way, like candy, nuts, fruit, and cheese—eat twice as much as you usually do. Remember to drink before you are thirsty and eat before you are hungry. Whatever you bring, remember to pack out all your trash. Other essentials for your pack include a map, sunscreen, lip balm, sunglasses, and a first-aid kit (or just a few bandages to take care of any scrapes and cuts, along with some moleskin to help with blisters). Sometimes a hike lasts longer than you expect, so instead of having to find your way back to the rim in the dark, pack a flashlight. Just because you bring a cell phone, it doesn't mean it will work in the canyon—you must be responsible for your own safety!

Depending upon your interests, you can bring along other items that will make your adventures more interesting, such as field books, binoculars, and a camera. If you plan to hike off-trail, a compass, fire starter, signal mirror, knife, and police whistle are vital tools; just make sure you know how to use them before you embark on your hike.

131

You can usually escape the crowds by hiking the North Rim or into the canyon—anywhere away from the South Rim's main visitor areas. And while you're awestruck by one of the world's great wilderness areas, don't forget to take some basic precautions to make your hike a fun and safe experience.

Summer weather in the Grand Canyon is, at best, extremely hot and dry. When you combine the extreme heat with the ruggedness of the terrain, you get dangerous conditions that may result in heat exhaustion, dehydration, and heat stroke. It's best to plan your hike during the cooler seasons of spring or fall. If summer is your only option, try to avoid the high temperatures by following some important guidelines:

- Consider hiking the rim trails, which can be about 20–30 degrees cooler than the canyon floor. Canyon temperatures can reach 110°F in the shade, and shade is in short supply!

- Overnight hikers into the canyon should begin their trip, their daily changes of camp, and their return hike to the rim before 7:30 A.M. or after 4 P.M.

- Wear a hat, sunscreen, sunglasses, and light clothing that covers the body.

- Take along clothes that you can layer; include wind- and water-resistant outer clothing.

- Hiking during midday (10 A.M.–4 P.M.) is not recommended.

- Protect your skin and eyes from the sun, wear light but supportive footwear, and pack lightly (but don't forget safety items).

- Hyponatremia mimics the early symptoms of heat exhaustion—nausea, vomiting, frequent urination, and disorientation. This is a result of low sodium content in the blood due to drinking too much water without consuming enough salt. Have the victim rest and eat salty foods. If their condition does not improve get immediate help.

- Hypothermia can be a problem when nighttime temperatures dip down to freezing on the rim or when you're wet and exhausted during windy weather conditions in the Inner Canyon. Symptoms include uncontrolled shivering, poor judgment, and loss of muscle control. Drinking warm liquids, putting on dry clothes, and warming the victim with body contact can help control the symptoms. A well-prepared hiker is ready for the most unpredictable changes in weather. (See the *Quick Reference* chapter for a list of hiking and backpacking supplies.)

- Although rattlesnake bites are rare, scorpion stings happen more frequently. Take precautions when lifting wood or rocks, shake out sleeping bags, wear shoes, and check boots before dressing. If stung, apply cold compresses to relieve pain and monitor the wound. Rarely does a scorpion sting require evacuation or cause serious health problems. Avoid nests of red ants that can leave painful bites, and watch for the spines of cactus and agave plants.

- Even though river and stream water may look good enough to drink, there are certain organisms that can make you regret that first gulp. Giardia and campylobacter bacteria can cause mild to really painful intestinal distress. If you can't boil fresh water for 3–5 minutes, treat it with iodine or filter it (maximum effective filter pore size for giardia is five microns).

Off-trail hiking is often hazardous to people and to the fragile vegetation and cryptogamic soils of the canyon (brown, black, or gray-colored soils covered with a mixture of algae, moss, or fungi). Try to minimize your impact on the canyon. Although sections of the canyon trails can be difficult to follow, relocate the trail, even if it means backtracking. If you're hiking in an area without a trail, try to walk on hard surfaces like bedrock, boulders, or dry washes. When choosing a lunch or campsite, use previously used sites or areas with hard surfaces, like slickrock or gravel. Use established toilets where provided, and don't put your trash in them. Remember, carry all trash out with you (including toilet paper, ash, and charcoal).

If you want to learn more about hiking in the Grand Canyon, visit one of the Park's bookstores, and pick up a copy of the *Official Guide to Hiking the Grand Canyon* by Scott Thybony or the Grand Canyon National Park Trails topographic map.

We'd like an easy day hike. Any suggestions?

If you're looking for an easy trail that doesn't take you into the canyon and takes no more than 2–3 hours, the following chart will give you some suggestions. These popular hikes follow along the easier rim trails and won't wipe you out for the rest of the day. The trailheads are easy to find, with spectacular views and scenic photo spots, some picnic areas, and plenty of ways to hop onto other good trails. All of them are good for families with children.

Although these are considered easy hikes, there's really no such thing at the Grand Canyon. High temperatures, especially during the summer months, mean you have to take precautions to avoid heat exhaustion, heat stroke, or hypothermia. Here are some hiking tips that will help:

- Always allow more time than you think the hike will take.

- Eat high-energy and salty foods frequently.

- Drink lots of water (at least 0.5–1 quart of water every hour you hike in the canyon per person) to replace fluids, and be sure to have a salty snack every time you drink to balance your sodium.

- Stay cool by soaking your hat and shirt at water sources and by wearing sunscreen and sunglasses.

- Always seek shade, and avoid hiking during the hottest part of the day (10 A.M.–4 P.M.).

- Go slow, and avoid huffing and puffing by resting frequently. Take a 10-minute break every hour.

HIKE BY AREA	DISTANCE (ROUND-TRIP)	DIFFICULTY	STARTS FROM
SOUTH RIM			
Mather Point to Yavapai Observation Station	1 mile	easy	Mather Point
Pima Point to Hermits Rest	1.1 miles	easy	Pima Point
Grand Canyon Village Loop	3 miles	easy	any viewpoint in village
Hermit Road (West Rim Drive) *(You can walk one way and return via shuttle, or just walk between any two lookout points, then take the shuttle back. Shuttle may not operate year-round.)*	approx. 12 miles one-way	easy	West Rim Interchange
NORTH RIM			
Cape Royal Trail	0.6 mile	easy	Cape Royal parking lot
Bright Angel Point Trail	1 mile	easy	Grand Canyon Lodge
Transept Trail	3 miles	easy	Grand Canyon Lodge

How about some more challenging hikes?

These main corridor trails take you over the rims and into the canyon, except where indicated. They're tougher than the easy hikes, requiring more time and a lot more "oomph" to walk up out of the canyon. Families with children are welcome to have a go; just make sure you have the time to rest often, and take along plenty of water and snacks. Many of these treks will lead you to awesome scenery, and you'll get a chance to experience the canyon as never before.

Make sure you take a look at the hiking tips before starting your trek. That way, you can avoid having the experience of heat exhaustion, heat stroke, and hypothermia.

HIKE BY AREA	DISTANCE (ROUND-TRIP)	DIFFICULTY	STARTS FROM
SOUTH RIM			
Bright Angel Trail to 1.5-Mile Resthouse	3 miles	moderate	Bright Angel Trailhead
South Kaibab Trail to Cedar Ridge	3 miles	moderate +	South Kaibab Trailhead
Bright Angel Trail to 3-Mile Resthouse	6 miles	moderate +	Bright Angel Trailhead
Bright Angel Trail to Indian Garden	9.2 miles	moderate +	Bright Angel Trailhead
NORTH RIM			
North Kaibab Trail to Supai Tunnel	4 miles	moderate +	North Kaibab Trailhead
North Kaibab Trail to Roaring Springs	9.4 miles	moderate +	North Kaibab Trailhead
Uncle Jim Trail	10 miles	moderate (rim trail)	Ken Patrick Trail off North Kaibab Trailhead
Widforss Trail	10 miles	moderate (rim trail)	Widforss Trailhead (2 miles north of Grand Canyon Lodge)

Note: + more strenuous

137

What are some great butt-kicking hikes?

For those who like to get their hearts really pumping and feel the burn in their legs, here's a list of some strenuous wilderness trails that will happily oblige. You'll need to be in good shape and carefully plan your trip for these babies, but they'll pay you back with some spectacular scenery and a feeling of accomplishment once you're finished. All of these require multiday trips (2–3 days), and many have overnight backcountry camping sites along the way. Remember that a backcountry permit is required for all overnight backpacking, and most of these permits are reserved up to four months in advance! If you arrive without a permit, you may be able to get one through a daily waiting list at the Backcountry Information Center. Be sure you have the time, conditioning, and energy before embarking on these journeys, as all of them of them have strenuous uphill climbs.

Don't forget to take a look at the hiking tips, and it's probably a good idea to refer to the *Camping and Backpacking* chapter of this book. For more information on other hikes in the canyon, pick up a copy of *Official Guide to Hiking the Grand Canyon* by Scott Thybony.

You gotta be kiddin' me!

HIKE BY AREA	DISTANCE (ROUND-TRIP)	DIFFICULTY	STARTS FROM
SOUTH RIM			
Bright Angel Trail to Plateau Point	12.2 miles	strenuous	Bright Angel Trailhead
South Kaibab Trail to Phantom Ranch	13.8 miles	strenuous	South Kaibab Trailhead
Bright Angel Trail to Bright Angel Campground	18.6 miles	strenuous	Bright Angel Trailhead
Bright Angel Trail to Phantom Ranch	19.6 miles	strenuous	Bright Angel Trailhead
NORTH RIM			
Ken Patrick Trail	20 miles	moderately strenuous	North Kaibab Trailhead parking lot
North Kaibab Trail to Ribbon Falls	16.8 miles	strenuous	North Kaibab Trailhead
North Kaibab Trail to Phantom Ranch	28 miles	strenuous	North Kaibab Trailhead
North Kaibab Trail to Bright Angel Campground	29 miles	strenuous	North Kaibab Trailhead
INNER CANYON			
South Rim to North Rim	42 miles	strenuous	South or North Kaibab Trailheads
WESTERN GRAND CANYON			
Hualapai Hilltop to Supai Village	16 miles	strenuous	Hualapai Hilltop

Can We mountain bike in Grand Canyon?

The good news for mountain bikers is that you can ride on all paved and secondary roadways and the Greenway Trail. The bad news is that none of the roads are well suited for mountain biking and the traffic along the South Rim can be a biking nightmare. All park trails, off-road backcountry areas, service roads, and utility corridors are off limits to two-wheelers. There are numerous backcountry roads in the Kaibab National Forest around both the North and South Rims that lend themselves to both mountain biking and bike touring.

Unless an early snowstorm closes the roadways, your window for biking opportunities lasts May–October around the North Rim; the busy South Rim offers year-round biking, but fewer options. The best time to ride in the national forestlands surrounding the park is during the clear, cooler days of September and October, when traffic is lighter (especially on the North Rim).

The park's shoulderless roads can be a challenge for novice bikers. Add some snow and icy conditions in the spring, and it can be downright dangerous. Other hazards include heavy summer traffic, which usually results in at least a few bike-versus-car accidents each year. It's best to avoid peak traffic periods (mid-morning–late afternoon during our summer months) on the roads that serve the main points of interest in the park. Riding at the crack of dawn or in the late afternoon in the forests surrounding the North Rim can be awesome.

Guided mountain bike tours led by knowledgeable guides are offered by a variety of companies and cater to most ability levels. Depending on the company, tours usually provide a mountain bike, helmet, water

140

bottle, and instruction in biking techniques and trail etiquette. For a list of bicycle tour companies, refer to the *Licensed Outfitters* section of the *Quick Reference* chapter of this book.

Repair services and bicycle rentals are available in the Arizona communities of Flagstaff (80 miles from the park's south entrance) and Sedona (110 miles from the park's south entrance). Prices range $30–70 for a full-day rental and $25–50 for a half-day rental. Some shops include helmets, tool kits, and water bottles, but it's best to ask.

Before you ride off into the distance, here are a few rules and safety precautions:

- Bicycle riders on public roadways in Grand Canyon National Park must obey the same rules and regulations that apply to motorized vehicles.

- Bicycles are not allowed on any park trails or in off-road backcountry areas. Service roads and utility corridors are closed to bikes unless use is expressly permitted.

- Bicycles must exhibit a white light in front and a red light or reflector on the rear during periods of low visibility.

- Wear a helmet and high-visibility clothing.

- Ride single file. Riding abreast on a public roadway is prohibited.

- Pull over and allow motorists to pass if you are impeding traffic flow.

- Yield the right-of-way to hikers and horse riders if you encounter them.

- The maximum number of cyclists traveling in a single cluster may not exceed 15, and these clusters must be at least 0.5 mile apart.

Can we go on a river trip through the Canyon?

Absolutely. You'll be able to choose from a lot of options, including cruising speed and length of trip, but no matter how you tailor your journey along the river, you'll get a unique view of the one and only Grand Canyon. If you're looking for more relaxation than adventure, try the half-day, smooth-water raft trips through Colorado River Discovery (888/522-6644, www .raftthecanyon.com) starting in Page, Arizona. These trips, running March 1–November 30 of each year, are great for the entire family (kids aged 4 and up can join you). Adult fare is $76, and children 4–11 are $66, water or soda is provided on your trip. The company also offers a full-day row trip on Mondays, Wednesdays, and Sundays March–May and September–November. The day begins at 8 A.M., with a return at 5 P.M. Fees includes lunch and are $161 for adults and $151 for kids.

Hualapai River Runners (928/769-2210 or 800/622-4409, www.desination grandcanyon.com) offers one-day white-water raft trips that include lunch and transportation from Peach Springs. Prices run $350.96 for adults and $265.75 for children 8–11. Contact them to learn about their current pricing and schedules.

For the more adventuresome, there are many commercial river concessionaires that take visitors on white-water rafting expeditions down the Colorado in the Grand Canyon April–October. Trips vary in length 3–18 days. All embark from Lees Ferry, with the option of taking a partial trip starting or ending at Phantom Ranch. Some trips are motorized, and others are oar-powered. Rates vary depending upon length of trip and transportation costs. All equipment, facilities, and meals are provided. Keep an eye out for the occasional reduced rates for families, children, groups, and off-season travel.

For a list of the river companies, with addresses and telephone numbers, refer to the *Licensed Outfitters* section of the *Quick Reference* chapter of this book. Due to their popularity, you'll need to make reservations for these trips well in advance.

What do we need to know about white-water rafting down the Colorado in the park?

The first thing to know is that the stretch of the Colorado River that winds through the Grand Canyon offers some of the best white-water rafting opportunities and guided rafting trips in the world. Almost anyone, including those who are physically challenged, can take one of these trips.

All the river-rafting companies who lead trips on the Colorado have experienced guides, so don't worry if you don't have prior river experience. However, the rigors of outdoor life are not for everyone. There are inherent risks, and medical help is not readily available. Still, the safety records of our registered outfitters are excellent, and guides are well trained in first-aid and evacuation techniques. Since everyone wears a Coast Guard–approved life jacket, there is little chance of trouble should you fall in the river. While swimming ability is recommended, many non-swimmers take these trips each year.

On most of the trips, you're on the raft 4–8 hours a day. Trip itineraries usually include daily stops at beaches, scenic side canyons, and points of interest, with many opportunities to hike, swim, and just relax. Each day, your guides will set up camp, complete with a kitchen and portable toilet. Good hearty meals (some companies offer vegetarian) are included.

Depending upon the time of year, camping along the river has many benefits. The weather is warmer, and there are fewer insects. The best months for rafting through the Grand Canyon are May, September, and October, when the average high temperature is 82°F, and the average low is 57°F. During the spring and fall, it may feel like you have the river to yourselves (a "no-motors" period begins after September 15). During June, July, and August, daytime temperatures frequently exceed 100°F, although the humidity is low and there is a natural cooling effect while on the river. Expect rain any month, though afternoon thundershowers are most likely July–mid-September.

While you're on the Colorado River, you may see some experienced river runners (besides your guides). You can have a great time watching them go down the large rapids.

Refer to the *Licensed Outfitters* section of the *Quick Reference* chapter for a list of white-water rafting companies. Remember, a visit to websites can be very informative. When you make your reservations, be sure to ask about what is and isn't included in the trip, as that can vary from company to company.

The Colorado River Through the Grand Canyon: World-Class River Running

RIVER FACTS

- Length: 277 river miles through the canyon
- Average width: 300 feet
- Minimum width: 75 feet at Middle Granite Gorge (river mile 135)
- Average depth: 40 feet
- Greatest depth: 85 feet
- Average gradient: 8 feet per mile

Elevation of river:
- Lees Ferry (east end of canyon): 3,116 feet
- Lake Mead (west end of canyon): 1,200 feet

Average annual precipitation:
- Lees Ferry: 5.8 inches
- Lake Mead: 4.6 inches
- Phantom Ranch: 8.4 inches (historically, ranges 3–15 inches)

Back in 1869, John Wesley Powell was the first explorer to go through the canyon on the Colorado River. Most of the points along the river were named by Powell. The following are some of the most difficult rapids along the 277-mile stretch of the river in the canyon (approximate river mile indicated):

- Badger Creek Rapid (Mile 8)
- House Rock Rapid (Mile 17)
- North Canyon Rapid (Mile 20)
- 24 and 25 Mile Rapid
- Cave Springs Rapid (Mile 25)
- Kwagunt Rapid (Mile 56)
- Unkar Rapid (Mile 72)
- Hance Rapid (Mile 77)
- Sockdolager Rapid (Mile 79)
- Zoroaster Rapid (Mile 84)
- Horn Creek Rapid (Mile 90)
- Granite Rapid (Mile 93)
- Hermit Rapid (Mile 95)

RIVER RUNNING ON THE COLORADO

- The first solo river-running trip down the Colorado in the canyon was made in 1937, with the first inflatable boat trip and commercial trip made in 1938. The first motorized run down the Colorado in the canyon was accomplished in 1949.
- The best place to watch river runners rigging their boats is Lees Ferry.
- Commercial river guides are usually friendly and don't mind answering a few questions.
- You can apply for a permit for a noncommercial river-running trip through the Grand Canyon through the Grand Canyon River Permits Office (Grand Canyon National Park, P.O. Box 129, Grand Canyon, AZ 86023, 928/638-7843 or 800/959-9164, fax 928/638-7844).

Can we go horseback riding?

High in the saddle, you can get a unique perspective of the Grand Canyon and surrounding lands without ever breaking a sweat. You'll also be part of a long park tradition, as virtually all of the early exploration of the Grand Canyon was done on horseback. There are no horseback trail rides inside park boundaries (for mule trips in the park, refer to the *Getting Around* chapter). However, there are several stables just outside the park that lead guided rides through forests and along both canyon rims.

South Rim

One- or two-hour rides are offered by Apache Stables (P.O. Box 158, Grand Canyon, AZ 86023, 928/638-2891 or 928/638-3105, www.apachestables.com) in Kaibab National Forest on Highway 64, just outside the south entrance to the park. These unforgettable rides take you along trails that wander through the ponderosa pines of Kaibab National Forest. Cost is $45.50 for the one-hour ride (offered year-round), $85.50 for the two-hour ride. From May until the first cold spell in late fall, these stables also offer twilight campfire trail rides as well as wagon rides. These rides include a one-hour evening amble on a horse or a horse-drawn wagon, ending with a western campfire (all return by wagon). Costs are $55.50 for the trail/wagon ride and $25.50 for just the wagon ride. Reserve well in advance.

Western Grand Canyon (outside park boundaries)

If you have at least three days, you can try a saddle and packhorse trip into one of the most remote and beautiful corners of the southwestern part of the Grand Canyon. The trail starts at Hualapai Hilltop, 66 miles from Peach Springs on old Highway 66. You'll ride eight miles through stunning canyon scenery along Havasu Canyon Trail to the village of Supai on the Havasupai Indian Reservation. Here you'll find lodging and food services, as well as some of the canyon's most beautiful waterfalls. The cost of the saddle and packhorse trip from the Hualapai Hilltop Trailhead to the village of Supai and back is $120. The cost of a round-trip from the trailhead to the camp-ground, which is located two miles below Supai Village, is $150 (packhorses carry all equipment). For more information, contact the Havasupai Tourist Office (928/448-2121, 928/448-2141, 928/448-2174, or 928/448-2180) or the Havasupai Lodge (928/448-2111 or 928/448-2201). The lodge also offers day-time guided trail rides to Havasu Falls for $60 per person.

Forget about hiking. Some of the best trout fishing in the country, complete with easy boat access, is located at Lees Ferry, at the park's northeastern boundary. The more adventuresome can try a long hike down the canyon or a raft trip down the Colorado to one of many small tributary streams. At the western boundary of the park, on the Hualapai Indian Reservation, you'll find more good fishing by boat in the Lower Granite Gorge and Lake Mead areas.

Although fishing in the Grand Canyon can be done all year long, the best time of year is generally during the fall and winter. During those seasons, there are fewer people, cooler weather, and lower water levels at Glen Canyon Dam.

Anglers 14 years and older are required to have an Arizona fishing license. You can purchase one at the Camping Department of the Delaware North Park Services General Store at Market Plaza in Grand Canyon Village on the South Rim. You can also purchase fishing licenses before you arrive in the Park through the Arizona Game and Fish Department (866/462-0433, www.azgfd.gov). You'll also need a backcountry use permit for any overnight hiking or rafting jaunts into the canyon. The cost of the license varies. If you're a non-resident of Arizona, you can get a five-day permit for $32, a one-day license for $17.25, or an annual non-resident license for $63, including a trout stamp. If you're an Arizona resident, you'll pay $53 for an annual license with a trout stamp.

Along with ensuring a fun and fruitful fishing trip for you, the park's fishing regulations are crucial to the Grand Canyon's ecosystem. For instance, along the 16-mile stretch of prime fishing habitat from Lees Ferry to Glen Canyon, anglers are only allowed to fish with barbless hooks, flies, and lures; no bait allowed. We also have strict limit regulations that allow each angler to catch and keep two fish a day that measure under 16 inches. Any fish over 16 inches must be returned to the river unharmed to help encourage a bigger-size fish population.

Where are the best fishing spots?

Let's take a look at the options you have for fishing the waters of the Grand Canyon.

Lees Ferry

Some of the best fishing at the Grand Canyon is along the 16-mile stretch of the Colorado River on the eastern end of the Grand Canyon between Lees Ferry and Glen Canyon. More than half of the park's landed fish are caught here. Lees Ferry is accessible by paved road off Highway 89A and is located 84 miles from the park's north entrance and 127 miles from its south entrance. There are two fishing outfitters who can get you on the river. Located near Lees Ferry, Marble Canyon Lodge (928/645-9235 or 800/533-7339, www.lees-ferryflyfishing.com) provides anglers with guides, boats, and fishing equipment. Lees Ferry Anglers (928/355-2261 or 800/962-9755, www.leesferry.com) is a complete fishing outfitter, offering day trips that include guides, boats, fuel, and lunch. You'll be taken to some of the best fishing holes along this stretch of the river and get tips on catching the area's most plentiful species of trout: the rainbow (some measure close to 24 inches). There are some pretty strict regulations for fishing along this stretch of the Colorado. Check with the Backcountry Office (928/638-7875) for more information.

Phantom Ranch

To get to the fishing holes around Phantom Ranch in the Inner Canyon, you'll have to hike or take a mule ride down Bright Angel Trail. Once you're at the Ranch, you'll have lots of opportunities for a chance at a rainbow, as you dip your line in Bright Angel Creek or the Colorado River. Some basic fishing supplies are available for guests of the Ranch. All you need to bring is your own pole, reel, and maybe some bait. Call Grand Canyon National Park Lodges (Xanterra, 303/297-2757 or 888/297-2757, www.grandcanyonlodges.com) for more information.

Lake Mead

At the opposite end of the Colorado River from Lees Ferry, on the western end of the Grand Canyon, Lake Mead offers an unparalleled area for water recreation and fishing. The lake is famous for its striped bass (some as large as 40 pounds), but you can also catch largemouth bass. There are various marinas on the lake that rent boats, but you'll have to be your own guide. There's a public boat ramp at Meadview, which provides easy access to fishing in the lower Grand Canyon.

Winter in the Grand Canyon is a study in contrasts. While the roads to the South Rim remain open, the North Rim road is closed to all automobile traffic. You can enjoy cross-country skiing and snowshoeing along both the North Rim (most of the winter) and the South Rim (when there's enough snow). Inside the canyon you'll be treated to mild hiking weather and relatively empty trails and campgrounds. Visitors to the South Rim can enjoy all park programs including guided walks, talks, hikes, and tours (weather permitting), while the only way to access and enjoy the North Rim is via cross-country skis or snowshoes.

South Rim

Whether you can cross-country ski or snowshoe on the South Rim during the winter depends on how much snow there is. Conditions permitting, you can rent skis at the DNPS General Stores in Tusayan and Grand Canyon Village. You'll find groomed trails in the Kaibab National Forest near the Arizona Trail, east of Grandview Point. For hardy campers, Mather Campground stays open all year. For more information, call the Tusayan Ranger District Office (928/638-2443).

North Rim

The North Rim is a winter wonderland. While snow is usually plentiful, services are not. After the road to the North Rim closes with the first snow, you won't find any water, toilet, or other services except in Jacob Lake, 32 miles north of the park entrance. If you're still willing to give it a shot, you'll need to get a backcountry permit—call 928/638-7875—and be conditioned for long-distance skiing. The Jacob Lake Campground is open, minus any facilities. Remember, snowmobiles are not allowed inside park boundaries. There's also cross-country skiing throughout the Kaibab National Forest lands around the North Rim. Call the North Kaibab Ranger Station (928/643-7395) in Fredonia, Arizona for more information.

Inner Canyon

Winter inside the canyon is one of the park's best-kept secrets, a real treat for the more adventuresome visitors. Although you may have to gear up by adding crampons to your boots as you hike down ice- or snow-covered trails, once you're inside the canyon the weather is mild, the trails are empty, and the camping superb. Between November and March, reservations for a mule trip down to Phantom Ranch, through Xanterra Parks and Resorts (303/297-2757 or 888/297-2757, reserve-gcsr@xanterra.com, www.grandcanyonlodges.com), are easier to get, and the weather isn't as hot. For an unforgettable backpacking experience, you can camp at any of the backcountry campgrounds inside the canyon.

·The Future of the Grand Canyon·

As a World Heritage Site, the Grand Canyon is recognized as a place of universal value, containing natural and cultural features that should be preserved as part of the heritage of all people. Because it is one of the most popular national park sites in the world, it has become increasingly difficult to control the impact created by over four million annual visitors and their cars on the few developed areas along the rims. This is especially true of the South Rim, where most of the visitation in the park occurs. The roads and facilities were never designed to handle this volume of use, resulting in a gradual degradation of the visitor experience and negative impacts on the park's natural and cultural resources.

Future planning for the park focuses on improving orientation and identification services, improving traffic flow, increasing employee housing, preserving the rustic character of the Park structures, and improving pedestrian circulation at various points around the park.

Some suggestions put forth in development plans, some of which have already begun implementation, include:

- Establishing an orientation kiosk about the Walhalla Plateau to encourage visitors to travel the road to Cape Royal and Point Imperial and provide other pertinent information on services and opportunities on Bright Angel peninsula on the North Rim.

- Expanding parking area at the North Kaibab Trailhead.

- Establishing a seasonal work camp for Park employees and volunteers in the North Rim area.

- Rehabilitation and re-use of historic buildings for administrative buildings and housing.

- Enhancing visitor center exhibits, slide programs, and visitor lodging at the Grand Canyon Lodge.

· Ranger's Farewell ·

I hope that I've answered all of your questions about the Grand Canyon and that you've learned some inside information on ways to make your visit to the canyon more enjoyable.

The next chapter in the book is called *Quick Reference.* It's filled with lots of easy-to-find facts, forms, and information about the canyon. The subjects are in alphabetical order so you can quickly find what you need without having to thumb through the whole handbook. My favorite is a Grand Canyon timeline that answers questions that we may not have covered in the rest of the book.

Good hunting, and be sure to let us know if we need to change anything to improve future versions of this book. You can write to:

Susan Frank, c/o Avalon Travel
1700 Fourth Street
Berkeley, CA 94710

Bye for now,
Ranger Jack

Quick Reference

AREA VISITOR ATTRACTIONS

Grand Canyon National Park is the centerpiece of four major national park-land and recreation areas, including (from north to south) Canyonlands National Park, Glen Canyon National Recreation Area, Grand Canyon National Park, and Lake Mead National Recreation Area. Together, they stretch across some 400 miles, as the raven flies, of the most remote and beautiful wildlands in the world, and over 800 miles along the mighty Colorado River. There are also five tribes, or nations, of American Indians that have reservations near Grand Canyon National Park. In other words, you'll be visiting an area rich in natural wonders and cultural treasures. To get the most out of your trip, you might want to visit some of the following area attractions.

The Arboretum at Flagstaff (928/774-1442, www.thearb.org). Here you'll see over 2,500 species of high-elevation plants, all native to Northern Arizona. As you walk through the center, you'll learn about the area's native, experimental, and exotic plant species, and their uses. Guided tours are available and you may see several of the 100 species of birds sighted in the area.

Canyon de Chelly National Monument (928/674-5500, www.nps.gov/cach). Visit ancient Native American ruins from the Great Pueblo period, and see sheer sandstone walls that soar a thousand feet into the air to create amazing vistas.

Grand Canyon Skywalk (702/878-9378 or 877/716-9378, www.grandcanyonskywalk.com). Commissioned by the Hualapai Indian tribe, this tourist attraction was unveiled in March 2007. For a $25 fee, you can walk on a glass horseshoe-shaped walkway 4,000 feet over the Colorado River. Visitor buildings and restaurants are in the works.

Lake Powell and Glen Canyon Dam (928/608-6072, www.glencanyon-nha.org). A national recreation area covering over 1,800 square miles of natural beauty, Glen Canyon Dam lies near Page, Arizona, at the border of Northern Arizona and Utah. Take a free, guided 45-minute tour of the dam, or enjoy all forms of water recreation along the 186-mile-long Lake Powell.

Lowell Observatory, Flagstaff (928/774-3358, www.lowell.edu). Founded in 1894, this observatory has become one of the country's leading astronomical institutions, offering some of the clearest viewing fields in North America. Maybe that's why the first observations of Mars were made here, leading to the discovery of Pluto in 1930. You can take a tour, view the telescope, and watch multimedia shows.

Meteor Crater (928/289-5898 or 800/289-5898, www.meteorcrater.com). This enormous crater measures nearly a mile wide and over 550 feet deep and closely resembles the surface of the moon. The crater is a NASA-designated training ground used by U.S. astronauts. Visit the Visitor Center to watch the *Collisions and Impacts* movie to learn more about this unique site.

Montezuma Castle National Monument (928/567-3322, www.nps.gov/moca). Located in Verde Valley, just off Interstate 17, this national monument features one of the best-preserved cliff dwellings in the country. Explore the five-story, 19-room ruin and Montezuma's Well.

Monument Valley Navajo Tribal Park (928/672-2366, www.navajonationparks.org). Located near the Utah border, Monument Valley is best known for the dramatic landscape of dunes, sandstone spires, and buttes that has been the backdrop for countless Hollywood films. Various tours of the monument, including jeep and horseback, are available by commercial guides. Check at the visitor center for a list and for road conditions.

Museum of Northern Arizona, Flagstaff (928/774-5213, www.musnaz.org). A visit to the Grand Canyon wouldn't be complete without a visit to this museum, which features the most extensive collection of Native American art and artifacts in the country. Located on Highway 180 just north of Flagstaff, it offers exhibits that explore all facets of the fascinating Southwest American Indian cultures.

Oak Creek Canyon, Sedona. This area has become a vacation haven for visitors from across the country. Discover the dramatic scenery of red rock landscapes and the treasures of Sedona, including art galleries, golf courses, and lots of outdoor recreational activities.

Sunset Crater and Wupatki National Monuments (Sunset Crater 928/556-7134, www.nps.gov/sucr; Wupatki 928/679-2365, www.nps.gov/wupa). The site of an ancient Anasazi ruin, Wupatki reveals secrets about the unique culture that thrived in the area for over 150 years. Located just 10 minutes away, Sunset Crater is a lava flow frozen in time, from an eruption that took place some 900 years ago.

Tuzigoot Ruin National Monument (928/634-5564, www.nps.gov/tuzi). Located near Cottonwood, Arizona, this village site is believed to have been abandoned by Native Americans sometime around A.D. 1400.

Walnut Canyon National Monument (928/526-3367, www.nps.gov/waca). An intricately built and well-preserved example of some 300 small cliff rooms built into the canyon's limestone walls. Located just outside Flagstaff, this is a great place to see ruins that are relatively close to a trail.

CHECKLIST FOR WILDERNESS CAMPERS AND BACKPACKERS

Clothes
- Sturdy hiking shoes or lightweight boots that are broken-in
- Thick hiking socks
- Shorts, jeans, fleece pants, and sweatshirt
- Cotton T-shirt or long-sleeved shirt
- Rain-resistant jacket, poncho, and pants
- Warm hat and gloves
- Set of extra clothes (T-shirt, a long-sleeved cotton shirt, and a down vest or light jacket)
- UV protection sunglasses

Equipment
- Rain-resistant sleeping bag and pad
- Backpacking tent and stakes
- Frame backpack (for longer hikes and overnight trips)
- Flashlight/headlamp (carry fresh batteries and a spare bulb)
- Water bottle (at least quart-size)
- Backpacking stove and fuel
- Cooking pot, cup, and utensils
- Fire starter kit (waterproof matches in waterproof container, candle, and dry paper)
- Topographical map and compass
- Pocketknife
- Watch
- Water purification device

Supplies
- Water (at least 0.5–1 quart of water for each hour of hiking per person and more for cooking and cleaning)
- Water purification tablets
- Sunscreen, insect repellant, lip balm
- Small first-aid kit with blister kit
- Toilet items
- Mirror or other reflective item for signaling
- Food (also carry emergency rations like raisins, nuts, hard candy, etc.)
- Miscellaneous (large bandana, extra closeable plastic bags for keeping items dry and packing out your trash)

CHRONOLOGY OF GRAND CANYON'S CULTURAL HISTORY

A.D. 1–700   The earliest farmers were the ancestral Pueblo people, or Anasazi, from a Navajo word meaning "Ancient Ones." This term included both the Basketmakers and Pueblo Indians. The Basketmakers were so called because of the variety of beautiful, well-made baskets that they produced, using twisted and coiled grass and yucca leaves. By A.D. 600, the Basketmakers had also learned to make pottery, baked for durability.

700   Major changes occurred in the Basketmaker way of life. Pueblo villages were independent, like Greek city-states. Rules and customs became highly developed. Reflecting their agricultural way of life, the Pueblos' religion sought rain in a dry land and fertility for life-sustaining crops. Elaborate ceremonies included masked and costumed dancers. With pictographs and murals, they decorated the walls of kivas (special rooms for religious purposes), caves, and cliffs.

1000–1100   Pueblo occupation of the Grand Canyon area accelerated until there were hundreds of inhabited sites on the plateaus and in nooks and crannies of the canyon, from rims to river. During this time, the canyon was home to the most extensive human population in its entire history.

600–1150   The Coconino Plateau, Havasu Canyon, and parts of the Grand Canyon south of the river were occupied by an agricultural and hunting people called Cohonina. This early culture flourished in the area until its disappearance around 1150, near the time of Pueblo abandonment.

1000–1400   The Apache and the Navajo tribes (then closely associated peoples) migrated southward across mountains and plains. They came as nomads, hunting and raiding. Finally they settled near the Pueblo Indians and raided them at times.

1150–1200   Pueblo Indians almost completely abandoned the Grand Canyon.

1540   White men saw the Grand Canyon for the first time. The discovery was an incident in the search for the Seven Cities of Cibola by Francisco Vásquez de Coronado. García López de Cárdenas, a young soldier in the expedition, is recognized as the Spanish discoverer of the Grand Canyon. The place where Cárdenas and his men first saw the Grand Canyon is not known. The point that best fits his description is the area between Moran Point and Desert View.

1776 Francisco Garces was a missionary who searched for new American Indian tribes in order to win their allegiance for his church and king. On June 20, 1776, he came into the deep canyon of the Rio Jabesua (Havasu, or Cataract Creek). Garces was the first writer to refer consistently to the Rio Colorado and named the Grand Canyon, Puerto de Bucareli. He set out for the Hopi pueblos on June 25, 1776. On the following day, he viewed the Grand Canyon, which he perceived as an endless series of canyons, within which flowed the Rio Colorado (Red River).

1803 With the Louisiana Purchase, the young United States of America became the northeastern neighbor of New Spain.

1821–1848 The Grand Canyon was within the territory of an independent Mexico.

1824 While still part of Mexico, the Grand Canyon was first visited by men from the United States. There was very little Mexican supervision in the canyon and plateau country around the Grand Canyon, so mountain men traveled there pretty much as they pleased, searching for beaver and other furs.

1825 William Henry Ashley, one of the leading fur traders, descended the upper Green River through several of its canyons, distinguishing himself and his six men as the first to attempt a boat trip down the Colorado's "mainstream."

1848 The Grand Canyon region became United States territory as a result of the Mexican War, which was ended by the Treaty of Guadalupe Hidalgo, ratified on May 30, 1848. Also in 1848, gold was discovered in California, providing the impetus for increased travel along routes to the gold fields, passing both north and south of the Grand Canyon.

1850 The Territory of New Mexico, which included Arizona and the Grand Canyon, was created.

1857 The War Department authorized Lieutenant Joseph Christmas Ives to explore the Colorado River "to ascertain how far the river was navigable for steamboats." The expedition's artists, F. W. von Egloffstein and H. B. Mollhausen, were the first to sketch the Grand Canyon, although their sketches appear dark and forbidding and fail to convey an impression of its beauty. Dr. John Strong Newberry, a geologist, also accompanied the expedition and had the honor of being the first scientist to study Grand Canyon, "the most splendid exposure of stratified rocks that there is in the world."

1863	Abraham Lincoln signed the bill establishing Arizona Territory.
1867 (pproximate date)	The Navajo tribe signed a peace treaty with the United States and were allowed to return to their traditional lands. The reservation then established was later expanded to include sections of the eastern Grand Canyon in 1884, 1900, and 1930.
1868	The first map containing "Grand Canyon" as a place name accompanied General William J. Palmer's railroad survey report.
1869	The Hualapai made peace with the U.S. Army, and many of their warriors served as scouts for General George Crook in his campaign against their traditional enemies, the Yavapai.
1869	Major John Wesley Powell began his exploration of the Grand Canyon. He played a leading role in the second "opening" of the West—its opening to science, conservation, and coherent use. When he completed his work, the Colorado River's path was known, its vast canyons named and measured, their ancient book of geology laid open for scientific study, and the civilization of the Native American inhabitants, ancient and modern, recorded for posterity. Powell's expedition came upon the mouth of a clear, cold stream. He named it Bright Angel. The honor of the first consistent and authoritative use of the name "Grand Canyon" belongs to Major Powell, whose definitive and widely read reports caused the name to be adopted permanently.
1870	Powell explored the plateaus north of the Grand Canyon to locate supply routes for his second river expedition.
1870–1880	Copper mining districts were opened near the Grand Canyon, in the Grand Wash Cliffs and Mt. Trumbull

areas. In order to provide themselves with a supply of pack animals (burros are not native to America), prospectors released burros into the canyon, where they thrived on the sparse vegetation and multiplied. Although some burros were lost, the population increased until, in modern times, it reached an estimated 2,000. Much destruction of plant cover and fouling of springs resulted.

1870–1890 Ranchers, settlers, and colonists arrived in the Grand Canyon region. Arizona Territory quadrupled its non–American Indian population, from under 10,000 to over 40,000 and more than doubled it again, to 88,000, by 1890. In that year the U.S. Bureau of the Census declared the frontier at an end.

1871 Powell's second Colorado River expedition left Green River, Wyoming. John Doyle Lee, a controversial Mormon, moved to the crossing of the Colorado River at the mouth of the Paria River. He established a ferry there, and it has been called Lees Ferry ever since.

1872 Powell's second expedition resumed their river trip from Lees Ferry and ended at Kanab Creek. During that summer, Powell explored the Kaibab Plateau and the North Rim of the Grand Canyon.

1873 With a new boat called the Colorado, Lee instituted regular ferry service, with a charge of $3 per wagon and $0.75 per animal.

1874 Most of the Hualapai people were removed to a reservation on the lower Colorado River, but the Havasupai tribe and the plateau tribes near the Grand Canyon remained.

1880 A proclamation by President Rutherford B. Hayes established the Havasupai Indian Reservation. This area, which was 5 miles wide and 12 miles long, surrounded the village and the cultivated portion of the canyon.

1880–1881 Clarence Edward Dutton of the new United States Geological Survey led a full-fledged geological expedition that resulted in the first important geological book on the Grand Canyon, *The Tertiary History of the Grand Canyon District, with Atlas.*

1882	The tracks for the Atlantic and Pacific Railroad were laid. The railroad followed a route surveyed by General William J. Palmer in 1867–1868, passing near the San Francisco Peaks and Bill Williams Mountain. Railroad camps such as Flagstaff, Williams, and Peach Springs were established. By 1883, the stop at Peach Springs on the Hualapai Reservation was the closest the railroad came to the Grand Canyon, and tourists began to make the 20-mile journey to the canyon fairly often.
1882–1883	Geologist Charles Doolittle Walcott traveled with Powell into the Grand Canyon. In order to take in its horses and equipment, this expedition enlarged the Nankoweap Trail, leading down into the eastern end of the canyon along the route of an old Native American trail.
1883	The area of the present Hualapai Reservation was set aside, and this was confirmed by order of President Chester A. Arthur.
1883	"Captain" John Hance arrived at the Grand Canyon and became the first white resident. He was a memorable story-teller, tourist guide, trailbuilder, and miner. He built a log cabin at the head of the Old Hance Trail. The first tourists known to have visited John Hance at the Grand Canyon were Edward Everett Ayer and his family and friends.
1885	Hance hired Philip and William Hull, who had a sheep ranch south of the canyon, as guides. They made a trip to the bottom of the canyon, giving Mrs. Ayer the distinction of being the first white woman to make the descent on foot.
1886	Businessmen in Flagstaff began the campaign for a rail line by organizing the Flagstaff and Grand Canyon Railroad Company and running a survey, but financial backing could not be secured at that time.
1890	William Wallace Bass set up a camp on the South Rim near Havasupai Point and completed a road to Ashfork.
1890–1891	Peter D. Berry, along with Ralph and Niles Cameron, widened Bright Angel Trail, which had been an old Havasupai Indian track, as far as Indian Garden.
1891	Louis D. Boucher, "The Hermit," came to the Grand Canyon. He rode a white mule with a bell around its neck.

His home camp was at Dripping Springs. His Silver Bell Trail descended from the rim to Dripping Springs and then out around Columbus Point into Long (Boucher) Canyon. There he planted a splendid orchard and garden and grew grapes, oranges, figs, peaches, pomegranates and other fruits, and vegetables of every kind, including tomatoes, chilies, and cucumbers. He had 75 trees. This orchard was near the site of Boucher's copper mine, where tourists could stay in cabins.

1892–1893	Peter D. Berry built the four-mile Grandview Trail from Grandview Point down to his mine, called the Last Chance.
1893	Daniel L. Hogan located a claim for a gold mine 1,000 feet below Maricopa Point. Since he was an orphan, he named it the Orphan Mine. He and others built a trail down into that area from Horsethief Tank, which he had also constructed.
1893	The Grand Canyon was proclaimed a forest reserve by President Benjamin Harrison.
1894	Hance built the Red Canyon, or New Hance, Trail, when rockslides made the old trail unusable.
1894	A creek was named. Peter D. Berry and Ralph and Niles Cameron, along with James McClure, were traveling along the Tonto Platform between the Grandview Trail and the Bright Angel Trail. Ralph Cameron was ahead of the others. In a streambed he found an old Meerschaum pipe. He picked it up, scratched a date about 100 years previous on it and put it where the others could not miss it. His companions fell for the joke, speculating on who might have been there so long before. The story was too good not to tell. The stream has been called Pipe Creek ever since.
1894	The citizens of Williams contributed $1,000 to finance a survey for a railway.
1895	To finance a survey for a railway, Hance sold his ranch and trail to J. Wilber Thurber, who operated a stage line from Flagstaff. Hance continued to live at his ranch.
1896	The Bright Angel Hotel, an early tourist accommodation in Grand Canyon Village, was brought into service.
1896	BIA agent Henry P. Ewing was appointed to the Walapai

Indian Agency, which supervised both tribes. He began to collect fees for grazing and timber cutting on the reservation.

1897 Hance became the first postmaster on the rim of the Grand Canyon when the post office of Tourist, Arizona was established at Hance Ranch.

1897 The Santa Fe and Grand Canyon Railway Company was organized by Lombard, Goode and Company to build a railroad and telegraph line from Williams to the Grand Canyon. An act of Congress was required, granting right of way across the Grand Canyon Forest Reserve. The Grand Canyon was placed under the General Land Office of the Department of the Interior.

1898 Bright Angel Trail was extended down to the river.

1901 Peter D. Berry sold his Last Chance Mine to the Canyon Copper Company, an eastern consortium.

1901 The first scheduled train traveled from Williams to the Grand Canyon. The almost total lack of permanent surface water at the Grand Canyon was the most pressing problem in the development of the area. All water was hauled in railroad tank cars over distances of 60–120 miles.

1902 The first automobile known to make the trip to the Grand Canyon was a remarkable steam-driven automobile, a new Toledo eight-horse-power Locomobile. It chugged out of Flagstaff toward the Grand Canyon but ran out of gas 18 miles from the canyon. Pete Berry hauled gas from the railroad terminal to the machine, which was finally nursed up to the South Rim five days after it had left Flagstaff. The first automobiles to go to the North Rim were a Locomobile and a Thomas Flyer. They left Kanab in June 1909 and made the trip in three days. Gasoline had been cached in advance along the way.

1902 Ellsworth L. Kolb and Emery C. Kolb came to the Grand Canyon. The Kolb brothers became nationally known for their boat trip down the Colorado River in 1911–1912, which was the first to be recorded on motion picture film. Emery gave lectures on the river trips and the canyon for 60 years. He died in 1976, at age 95, and is buried beside his wife and brother in Pioneer Cemetery at Grand Canyon.

1902	Francois Emile Matthes began the first topographic map of the Grand Canyon. He began his map for the U.S. Geological Survey on the South Rim, establishing bench marks and using triangulation, leveling, and plane-table methods to establish the position and elevation of points that could be seen from the rim. During scorching days on the Hance Trail, the rocks became so hot that the men had to shift continually from one foot to the other to avoid burning. Matthes named Krishna Shrine, Solomon Temple, Wotan's Throne, and Walhalla Plateau.
1903	Theodore Roosevelt visited the Grand Canyon. He was deeply moved by the beauty of the canyon and remarked that it was "to me the most impressive piece of scenery I have ever looked at."
1903	Arthur R. Sanger, John A. King, and their boatman, E. B. "Hum" Woolley (all of whom were apparently miners) left Lees Ferry in August for a trek in their 18-foot oaken boat. By the end of October, they had reached Yuma.
1903	The Supai Post Office opened. This required the mail carrier to travel over a long, rough trail to the Havasupai Indian community in its alcove of the Grand Canyon.
1905	A first-class hotel, El Tovar, was opened. Combining the architectural flavors of a Swiss chateau and a castle on the Rhine, it was made of native boulders and Douglas fir logs. The building cost $250,000 to construct. It was named El Tovar in honor of the Spanish explorer who had visited the Hopi towns (but not the Grand Canyon) in 1540. A replica of an Hopi pueblo, called the Hopi House, was constructed nearby. John G. Verkamp had been running the first curio stand in a tent of the Bright Angel Hotel. In 1905, he built a curio store east of the Hopi House, which still exists.
1906	Martin Buggeln, former manager of the Bright Angel Hotel, bought Hance Ranch and built a white, 17-room frame hotel beside the old log dining room.
1906	The Grand Canyon Game Preserve was set aside, and soon afterwards James T. "Uncle Jim" Owens was appointed warden by the Forest Service.
1907	The bottom dropped out of the copper market. New

methods had been developed for processing low-grade ore, and the high-grade ore of the Last Chance Mine was no longer worth hauling out of the canyon.

1907	A cable crossing the river was installed at the mouth of Bright Angel Creek.
1908	Theodore Roosevelt declared portions of the Grand Canyon a National Monument.
1908	William Wallace Bass installed a cableway across the river at Bass Crossing, with a cage big enough to carry a burro. It was soon enlarged to permit a mule or horse to be sent across. Later, he built another cableway three river miles below, near the mouth of Hakatai Canyon. The cables remained in place until 1968, when they were removed as a hazard to aircraft.
1909	The first sportsman's river trip was made by Julius F. Stone, an Ohio manufacturer. Companions were Seymour S. Deubendorff and Nathaniel Galloway, who designed a boat that was decked-over, except for a cockpit in which a single oarsman sat. The trip from Green River, Wyoming, to Needles was made in only 10 weeks.
1910	The flood of 1910 swept away most of the homes, as well as the school, of the Havasupai Indian community. The first Master Plan for Grand Canyon was written by the U.S. Forest Service, who managed the Grand Canyon until 1919.
1914	Hermits Rest, a stone-and-log building where weary travelers could find refreshment, was built. The architect was Mary Colter.
1915	Neil M. Judd was the first professional archaeologist sent to investigate the Grand Canyon. The Bureau of American Ethnology hailed the proclamation of Grand Canyon National Monument as a means of protecting "innumerable antiquities, including cliff-dwellings, pueblos, dwelling sites, and burial places."
1916	The National Park Service was created, "To conserve the scenery and the natural and historic objects and the wildlife therein and to provide for the enjoyment of the same in such manner and by such means as will leave them unimpaired for the enjoyment of future generations."

1918	A monument to John Wesley Powell and the men of his two Colorado River expeditions was dedicated (it was built in 1916). The memorial is a truncated stone pyramid with a bronze plaque.
1919	President Woodrow Wilson signed the bill that created Grand Canyon National Park.
1919	The Hualapais elected a tribal council. They were encouraged by their agents to develop the extensive grazing lands in their reservation on the Grand Canyon's southern margin by building fences, charging grazing fees, and starting a herd of their own. They were troubled by the Santa Fe Railroad's claim to half those lands.
1919–1939	The National Park Service saw a clear need for many kinds of buildings as well as more roads. As soon as funds were available, construction began on administration buildings, residences, warehouses, a mess hall, a stable/garage, and a blacksmith shop. Many additional roads and buildings were built and improved during this period of intense construction.
1920	The Grand Canyon National Park was formally dedicated on April 30 in ceremonies at the Powell Memorial. The first director of the National Park Service, Stephen Tyng Mather, paid for many of the badly needed improvements in the early parks out of his own pocket. His memorial stands at Mather Point on the South Rim.
1926	Automobiles overtook the railroad as the most popular way to travel to the canyon.
1926	A "recycling" plant for reclaiming wastewater, which could be used for non-potable purposes, began operating. It was designed by M. R. Tillotson and continues to be regarded as an excellent example, far ahead of its time, of effective conservation of a precious resource.
1926	A considerable number of Havasupais found employment in Grand Canyon Village, both with concessionaire Fred Harvey and the National Park Service, which recognized their special status within the park. Many lived in a camp near Grand Canyon Village. But without medical attention, proper housing, or adequate water, the camp was a rural slum. In the mid-1930s, the National Park Service provided new cabins,

and the Bureau of Indian Affairs made arrangements with the resident physician to give medical care. The Havasupai children began to attend the Grand Canyon School.

1928   With the erection of a rigid suspension bridge to replace the old swinging bridge, the cross-canyon Kaibab Trail was finished to "high standard of pack animal construction." The eight cables were so heavy that 42 Havasupai Indians were hired to station themselves at intervals, lift the cable to their shoulders, and proceed down the trail like a gigantic centipede.

1928   A fine observation station/museum was erected at Yavapai Point through a grant by the Laura Spelman Rockefeller Foundation. The museum had fixed binoculars pointed at important locations in the canyon.

1928   The Union Pacific Railroad installed a powerhouse and pumping plant on Bright Angel Creek near Roaring Springs, bringing a dependable supply of water to the North Rim. That same year, the U.S. Government took over Bright Angel Trail.

1929   A new Park Headquarters was built in the new village area south of the railroad tracks.

1929   Airplane service first became available across the Grand Canyon.

1929   Marble Canyon Bridge was dedicated near Lees Ferry, making one- or two-day vehicle travel possible between the North and South Rims.

1930   Hermit Camp was abandoned when it was made redundant by the opening of the Bright Angel Trail to free travel and the construction of the new South Kaibab Trail and Phantom Ranch.

1931   The scarcity of surface water and increasing visitation necessitated the building of a pipeline from the waters of Garden Creek at Indian Garden to the South Rim.

1932   A new Grand Canyon National Monument was proclaimed by President Herbert C. Hoover. Toroweap was an area of over 300 square miles adjoining the national park on the west and extending 40 miles along the Colorado River.

1932	The Desert View Watchtower, designed by the inimitable Mary Colter, was erected at the end of Desert View (or East Rim) Drive.
1935–1936	Hoover Dam was completed, and Lake Mead National Recreation Area was established.
1936	Construction began on the second North Rim Lodge to replace the original building, which was destroyed by fire.
1937	A good approach road from the east, through Cameron and Desert View, was paved. This gave the South Rim two entrances. There were 300,000 visitors to the Grand Canyon during this year, and a Ford Tri-motor airplane flew the canyon on a regular basis.
1938	The approach road from Kanab, Utah was completely paved. The Navajo or Marble Canyon Bridge was also paved, reducing the distance from South Rim to North Rim to its present 215 road miles.
1944	During this war year, only 65,000 visitors came, and many of these were servicemen on trips arranged for their units.
1948	The states of the Upper Colorado River Basin recommended the Colorado River Storage Project, including dams in Glen Canyon and Echo Park. Conservationists kept Echo Park Dam out of the bill, protecting Dinosaur National Monument. But, when the gates closed in 1964, Glen Canyon Dam flooded a larger area, including many historic and prehistoric sites. The days of the spring flood and the untamed river were over.
1951	The Geological Survey discovered that the Orphan Mine lode was rich in uranium. The mine was put into production by the Golden Crown Mining Company three years later. With the advent of the Atomic Age, the Orphan became the only active mine in Grand Canyon National Park. It passed into NPS hands in 1987.
1955	Construction began on new facilities at the South Rim as part of the National Park Service Mission 66 program.
1956	There were one million visitors to the park, and reservations were required.

1956	One of commercial aviation's worst disasters took place. Near noon on a reasonably clear day in June, two airliners on eastward flights from Los Angeles collided over the canyon and fell into the gorge near the river, killing all 128 people aboard. This collision resulted in the establishment of a national air traffic control system.
1960	The largest fire in Grand Canyon history, the Saddle Mountain Blaze, took place. It destroyed about 9,000 acres, mostly in the Kaibab National Forest but including 300 acres of parkland.
1964	Glen Canyon Dam began electrical generation.
1964	900 people ran the Colorado River.
1969	There were over two million visitors, yet the Vietnam crisis caused the government to cut appropriations for staff and facilities.
1970	Construction was completed on a pipeline that ran from Roaring Springs below the North Rim all the way down Bright Angel Canyon, across the river on a new suspension bridge, and up to the pumping station at Indian Garden by gravity flow.
1970	Nearly 10,000 people ran the Colorado River.
1972	Visitation reached 2.7 million but declined in the next two years due to fuel shortage and rising costs brought about by the Middle East conflict.
1974	An epoch on the Colorado River ended when Emery Kolb made his last trip in Grand Canyon, at the age of 93, as a passenger on Dock Marston's boat. His journey took him from the Little Colorado River to Crystal Rapid.
1975	The Historic District was established, and Hopi House was included in the district. The Grand Canyon Enlargement Act added Marble Canyon National Monument, and Grand Canyon National Monument, to Grand Canyon National Park.
1976	Visitation to the Grand Canyon passed three million.
1979	Grand Canyon National Park was designated a World Heritage Site.

1980–1981	After 17 years, Lake Powell was filled.
1980–1981	Fund for Animals removed feral burros from the Grand Canyon.
1983	A record post-dam flood scoured the canyon. Some rapids became impossible, stranding river trip passengers temporarily.
1989	Rail passenger service to the South Rim of the Grand Canyon was restored by owners of the new Grand Canyon Railway.
1992	The Grand Canyon Protection Act required operation of the Glen Canyon Dam to mitigate adverse impacts caused by widely fluctuating water levels in short periods on the Colorado River through Grand Canyon National Park.
1994	Grand Canyon celebrated its 75th anniversary as a national park.
1995	The General Management Plan for Grand Canyon was released with the goals of significantly reducing the use of automobiles and improving the visitor experience in Grand Canyon National Park.
1996	Six California condors were released at Vermilion Cliffs as part of a reintroduction program for this endangered species.
1997	Secretary of the Interior Bruce Babbitt called for the removal of 80 percent of all automobiles from Grand Canyon National Park.
2000	To meet the goals of the General Management Plan, the first phase of a new transportation plan for Grand Canyon National Park was implemented. The plan provides for year-round shuttle service on the South Rim, and the development of a new transportation center near Mather Point on the South Rim.
2003	The first wild endangered California condor chick fledges through the efforts of the Peregrine Fund and the NPS. Since this was the first chick born in the wild in 100 years, this is a historic year for their recovery in Arizona.

EDUCATION AND PRESERVATION PROGRAMS

Grand Canyon National Park is challenged by increasing visitation. To protect and preserve the wild and unimpaired nature of the Grand Canyon for the future and to provide educational materials for visitors, several nonprofit organizations have been established. The Grand Canyon Association and the Grand Canyon National Park Foundation work in partnership with the National Park Service and each other to provide educational materials and opportunities for visitors to contribute to the Grand Canyon's preservation. The Grand Canyon Trust (GCT) is a conservation organization dedicated to protecting the resources and wildlands of the Colorado Plateau, including Grand Canyon National Park. In addition, the NPS operates an Environmental Education Program at the Grand Canyon that provides school, group, and individual learning experiences in the park. Here's more information about each organization, including how you can help in the effort to support Grand Canyon National Park for future generations.

The **Grand Canyon Association** (P.O. Box 399, Grand Canyon, AZ 86023, 928/638-2481 or 800/858-2808, gcassociation@grandcanyon.org, www.grandcanyon.org) is a nonprofit educational organization founded in 1932 to aid educational, historical, and scientific programs for the benefit of Grand Canyon National Park and its visitors. They have provided over $20 million in financial support to Grand Canyon National Park since 1932. Contact the association to become a member or to get more information. Among other activities, the GCA:

- Operates bookstores in visitor centers throughout the park, with proceeds going to support park programs
- Founded the Grand Canyon Field Institute in 1993, which offers educational courses for all ages that enhance visitor understanding and enjoyment of the park through firsthand experience
- Publishes trail guides as well as more than two million pieces of free informational literature for park visitors each year
- Funds a variety of exhibits throughout the park
- Administers grants and gifts received for designated projects in the Grand Canyon
- Helps support wildlife surveys and scientific and cultural research through the Park's Science Center
- Provides continued support to Grand Canyon's research library through purchase of materials and employment of staff

- Organizes curriculum workshops for teachers, and teaches children about Grand Canyon geology, ecology, and history

The **Grand Canyon National Park Foundation** (625 N. Beaver St., Flagstaff, AZ 86001, 928/774-1760, www.grandcanyonfoundation.org) is a nonprofit organization incorporated in 1995. It operates under an agreement with the National Park Service, with the goal of helping to preserve, protect, and enhance Grand Canyon National Park and to enrich each visitor's experience. The Foundation receives no federal funding and is not a membership organization. The park can no longer depend on federal appropriations, which are lagging behind the park's growing needs. To help, the Foundation funds important projects and programs in support of the park, including exhibits, wildlife restoration projects, restoration of historic buildings, help in building the new Greenway biking and pedestrian trails, and interpretive programs. Its funds come from the support of private citizens, foundations, and corporations; contact the foundation to make a donation.

The Grand Canyon Trust (2601 N. Fort Valley Rd., Flagstaff, Arizona 86001, 928/774-7488 or 888/GCT-5550, www.grandcanyontrust.org) is a national, nonprofit conservation organization founded in 1985, dedicated to the preservation and protection of the spectacular wildlands and resources of the Colorado Plateau. Contact the trust to join. Some of their conservation projects include:

- Helping to preserve clean air for the canyon by working to get air pollution controls installed at several coal-fired power plants in the region

- Helping to preserve healthy forests by launching the Grand Canyon Forests Partnership, an ambitious project to restore 100,000 acres of ponderosa pine forests

- Cooperating with other groups to conduct extensive water use studies to help with future conservation projects

- Working to help manage the Glen Canyon Dam to benefit downstream natural resources

- Working to preserve the natural quiet and solitude of the canyon by controlling excessive air tours over the Grand Canyon

NPS Environmental Education Programs (928/638-7762, www.nps.gov/archive/grca/education) are operated by the NPS, which is always in the process of developing a variety of programs to help individuals, schools, and community groups learn more about the park and the need to protect park resources. These programs include:

- On-site, educational field trips

- Travel grants for schools
- School curriculum for teachers and teacher-training workshops
- Video loans to schools
- Area field trips
- An on-site environmental education center
- Environmental Youth Corps opportunities
- Junior Ranger programs in the Park
- Interpretive programs in schools with ranger visits or video conferencing
- College credit at Northern Arizona State University through the Grand Canyon Semester program
- Educational materials for international visitors
- Native American community education programs

Recycling. Grand Canyon National Park has instituted a comprehensive and successful park-wide recycling program for aluminum, glass, and plastic products. Park visitors are encouraged to deposit aluminum cans and glass in special receptacles located in all developed areas and campgrounds. Xanterra Parks and Resorts has also implemented a comprehensive recycling program throughout the park, which recycles newspapers, plastic, glass, and aluminum from all guest accommodations on a daily basis, and guest rooms contain recycled bathroom and paper products.

FAMILY ATTRACTIONS
AT THE GRAND CANYON

Interactive reading and exploring. The Grand Canyon Association (GCA) has a great selection of kids books and comics that help the youngsters learn about the Park while having fun reading! Stop by one of the GCA bookstores while you're in the park to find other selections for kids, including: *Rascal: The Tassel-Eared Squirrel* by Sylvester Allred; *Exploring the Grand Canyon: Adventures of Yesterday and Today* by Lynne Foster; *An Introduction to Grand Canyon Prehistory* by Christopher M. Coder; *Canyon Comics* by Mark Iacampo; and the illustrated *Desert Night Shift: A Pack Rat Story* by Conrad J. Storad. GCA bookstores are located throughout the park or visit www.grand-canyonassociation.org to order books.

Take a river-rafting trip. For an experience your kids will always remember, take them on a smooth-water (leisurely day of floating) or white-water (more exciting and active experience) rafting trip down the Colorado River. Most trips are offered spring–fall by Colorado River Discovery (888/522-6644, www.raftthecanyon.com). You can also visit the South Rim Visitor Center for more information on the smooth-water trip.

Take a hike or walk with a ranger. It's an easy hike from Yavapai Observation Station or the visitor center to Maricopa Point. You can try a self-guided nature trail or take a walk with a park ranger. Popular ones include searching for fossils on South Kaibab Trail and sunset nature hikes. Be sure to check *The Guide* newspaper for current schedules and locations.

Visit the Tusayan Indian Ruin and Museum. Explore the secrets left behind by the ancestral Pueblo people who lived in the Grand Canyon 800 years ago. Visit the museum to discover clues—pottery, drawings on rocks, split-twig figurines—that they left behind about how they lived.

Become a Junior Ranger. This popular program, designed for kids 4–14, helps young visitors learn about the care and protection of park resources by completing a list of fun activities. Pick up a copy of *Junior Ranger* at any visitor or information center in the park, and your kids will be on their way to earning a Junior Ranger certificate—ages 4–7 earn a Raven Award, ages 8–10 earn a Coyote Award, and ages 11 on up earn a Scorpion Award. Special Phantom Rattler Junior Ranger programs are available to those who visit Phantom Ranch. The months June–August offers three additional programs where kids can complete the Junior Ranger requirements: Adventure Hike/ Dynamic Earth, Discovery Pack, and one of the family programs, Way Cool Stuff for Kids or A Children's Reading Circle.

Visit the mule corral. Even though you may not be old enough to ride a mule into the canyon, it's great fun just to hang out in the morning at the mule Stone Corral at the head of Bright Angel Trail and watch the mule riders getting ready for the trip. Just remember to stay outside the corral.

Take a Field Institute day class. Make your visit to the canyon a family affair. The Grand Canyon Field Institute (GCFI) is a non-profit organization offering hiking, backpacking, and day classes in Grand Canyon National Park. The Institute conducts unique and fun-filled learning adventures designed for adults with children eight years of age or older unless otherwise indicated. GCFI is a program of the Grand Canyon Association.

Campfire programs. Come to a family campfire program to hear tales about prospectors and Native Americans, as well as stories about burros and bighorns. Check *The Guide,* or at any visitor center, for program times and locations.

Kid Discounts. Kids 16 years and under ride free on any canyon bus tour when accompanied by an adult family member. Contact Xanterra (888/297-2757, www.grandcanyonlodges.com), or for same-day reservations, call Xanterra South Rim (928/638-2631).

BACKCOUNTRY PERMITS: INFORMATION, DEADLINES, AND CONSTRAINTS

Canyon hikers are fully responsible for knowing and obeying all regulations. Backpackers are responsible for their own safety and for costs should a rescue be initiated. Please research carefully as you plan for a safe trip. Trail guides and maps may be purchased at www.grandcanyon.org.

Backcountry permits are currently $10, plus $5 per person per night (subject to change), and can be obtained up to four months in advance through the Backcountry Information Center. If you arrive without a permit and wish to get one, you can put your name on a waiting list by showing up at the Backcountry Information Center at 8 A.M. on the day you wish to hike. Your chances of getting a same-day permit is unlikely; you should plan for a 1–3 day (or longer) wait. The South Rim Backcountry Information Center is open daily for walk-in visitors 8 A.M.–noon and 1–5 P.M. MST. The North Rim Backcountry Information Center is open mid-May–mid-October for walk-in visitors 8 A.M.–noon and 1–5 P.M. MST. Advance reservations are highly recommended. To help you plan your visit, know that the busiest times to hike the canyon are spring, fall, and any school vacation period.

Every year, the requests for permits (30,000 for backcountry permits) far outweigh the allowed use limits (13,000 permits), which were established to protect the canyon and the quality of visitors' experience. For this reason, advance reservations are strongly recommended, and they can be made up to four months in advance. While the permit allows you access to the backcountry, it does not reserve a specific tent site within the backcountry.

There are three ways to apply for a permit:

- Bring your request in person to the Backcountry Information Center (preferred method).

- Fax your request to the Backcountry Information Center at 928/638-2125.

- Mail your request to the Backcountry Information Center, Grand Canyon National Park, P.O. Box 129, Grand Canyon, AZ 86023.

When sending in a permit request, the preferred method of payment is with a credit card. Be sure to indicate the maximum amount you authorize the Backcountry Information Center to charge so that your longest trip alternative can be considered. Valid personal checks and money orders against a United States bank are also accepted when made out for the correct amount. For more information, contact the Backcountry Office (928/638-7875, phone hours Mon.–Fri. 1–5 P.M. MST, except federal holidays, www.nps.gov/grca/planyourvisit/backcountry-permit.htm). At the website, you can also download a PDF of the permit application.

GRAND CANYON TRUST

Grand Canyon Trust (2601 N. Fort Valley Rd., Flagstaff, AZ 86001, 928/774-7488 or 888/GCT-5550, www.grandcanyontrust.org) is a national, nonprofit conservation organization dedicated to protecting and restoring the Grand Canyon region. Founded in 1985, the trust has an impressive track record of success. The Grand Canyon Trust is headquartered in Flagstaff, Arizona with a field office in Moab, Utah.

"The Grand Canyon Trust is one of the most effective conservation organizations I know. Through their work on some of the West's thorniest natural resource issues, they have shown an unequaled ability to get the job done."

—Stewart L. Udall, the 37th U.S. Secretary of the Interior

The Grand Canyon Trust works to preserve the slick rock canyons, spectacular landscapes, flowing rivers, and diversity of nature in the Grand Canyon and across the Colorado Plateau through these and other key projects:

- Clean air for the canyon. Air pollution controls are now installed at the Navajo power plant at the eastern end of the park, thanks to the trust's work.

- Healthy forests. The trust has launched the Grand Canyon Forests Partnership, an ambitious project to restore 100,000 acres of ponderosa pine forests.

- Restored Colorado River habitat. The trust works to manage Glen Canyon Dam to benefit downstream natural resources.

- Preserve natural quiet and solitude. The trust is fighting to control the number of sightseeing air tours over the Grand Canyon and is working for Congressional action to restrict noisy flights in all our national parks.

- Your contribution will help protect and restore the Grand Canyon for the next millennium. Membership prices range $35–1,000 and can be paid by credit card or check.

HISTORIC PEOPLE OF THE GRAND CANYON

Big Jim

A member of the Havasupai Indian tribe, "Big Jim" had the longest association with the Grand Canyon's pioneer era. For generations, maybe centuries, Big Jim's family (Vesna) held traditional rights to the acres surrounding the springs at Indian Garden, north of today's Grand Canyon Village and 3,000 vertical feet below the South Rim. Big Jim was born at these springs in the 1850s. Many Havasupai would spend summers away from the tribe's primary village in Havasu Canyon, enjoying the solitude of more remote areas with perennial springs. During the summers, Big Jim and his family would sleep in wickiups beside the springs, set wildfires to condition the soil, irrigate a small plot of peach trees and vegetables, and fill stacked-stone bins in nearby cliffs with emergency food supplies. Each autumn his family would climb up to the rim on a centuries-old footpath along natural breaks in the stone caused by the Bright Angel Fault, returning to their village in Havasu Canyon.

For nine decades, Big Jim interacted with the first white pioneers who came and eventually settled at the South Rim. He helped early settlers find their way in the area, moving between his summer home at Indian Garden and several winter homes on the rim. By the 1920s, he had become a headman among his people and a local celebrity among residents of Grand Canyon Village. A tall, stately man, he would often come to the village wearing a frock coat, top hat, and an official decoration given to him by King Albert of Belgium (a canyon visitor). Big Jim lived near the south-central rim of the Grand Canyon until the late 1940s.

John Wesley Powell

Like John Muir, Major John Wesley Powell was one of a distinctive group of self-taught 19th-century Renaissance men who traveled throughout the American West and wrote extensively about the experience. In 1869, he led the first organized expedition down 1,000 miles of the Colorado River, going through the Grand Canyon. It was a truly remarkable feat, accomplished in four small wooden boats and on meager rations. This was followed by a series of expeditions and the Powell Survey (1870–1874), during which he surveyed and mapped the Colorado River and its tributaries, naming virtually all the rapids and other features encountered along the river as it winds through the canyon. He is credited with giving the name "Bright Angel" to the area and with helping to build the Nankoweap Trail on the North Rim. Following his surveying work, this one-armed Civil War veteran founded the U.S. Geological Survey and the U.S. Bureau of American Ethnology. He was an early and ardent advocate of the wise use of water in the West and of Native American rights.

Captain John Hance

Captain John Hance was perhaps the Grand Canyon's most colorful resident and premier storyteller. He is said to have been the first white settler in the canyon, first visiting the South Rim before 1881 and staying until his death in 1919. Hance built a guest ranch in 1883 (Hance Ranch) and improved an old Havasupai trail along Hance Creek, three miles east of Grandview Point, to access his mining claims in the canyon. But after leading a prominent couple down into the canyon in 1884, he decided tourism would be a better source of income. In 1886, he built a cabin at the head of the trail and began to run advertisements inviting tourists to Hance Ranch. His tourist accommodations were rustic and had few comforts, but the expert guide and lifelong bachelor only charged $1 for a night's lodging, including dinner. He also rented complete camping outfits, including pack and saddle horses, trail clothing, and supplies. When a landslide covered the trail in 1894, Hance built a better one, known today as the New Hance Trail, which runs down Red Canyon east of his ranch. He became one of the canyon's most flamboyant storytellers, entertaining his guests with "whoppers" on a regular basis. He typically sported a full goatee and mustache and was seldom seen without a hat. He dressed in buckskins or in the turn-of-the-20th-century garb of prospectors. This polite and gentle man had an uncanny ability to hoodwink listeners with his legendary storytelling. Many of his tall tales are retold today by park rangers in campfire programs.

Mary Elizabeth Jane Colter

Mary Elizabeth Jane Colter was one of the rare women in the late 1800s who attended architectural school, worked as an architectural apprentice, and became a professional architect. In 1902, she was offered a job as a designer for the Fred Harvey Company, which was developing tourist properties along the South Rim of the Grand Canyon. This relationship was to last 46 years, resulting in seven historic South Rim structures and the only remaining Inner Canyon resort. Colter was fascinated by Southwestern Native American cultures and heritage, an interest that was reflected in such projects as the Watchtower at Desert View and the Hopi House. Her remarkable ability to highlight and reflect the natural beauty of the surrounding parklands is seen in such projects as Hermits Rest, Lookout Studio, Bright Angel Lodge, and Phantom Ranch. She also designed the interior of the El Tovar Hotel. At Phantom Ranch, look for the four cabins of mostly native stone and the north half of the lodge dining room to get a sense of her original design for this project, which cost $20,000 to build. Colter's buildings leave behind a rich architectural vernacular for the Grand Canyon.

William Owen "Bucky" O'Neill

A restless adventurer, newspaper owner, and local politician, "Bucky" O'Neill came to the South Rim area in the 1890s, looking for mining claims. When he discovered a long belt of copper deposits running south towards Williams, O'Neill decided that a railroad should be built from Williams to the South Rim, where he envisioned an area devoted to tourist facilities. It was because of O'Neill's tireless lobbying efforts, both locally and nationally, that the Santa Fe and Grand Canyon Railway was first formed in 1897, with "General" Bucky O'Neill and others as directors. In 1901, after the company suffered financing woes, the Santa Fe Pacific Railroad bought the nearly completed railroad and finished laying tracks under the name of the Grand Canyon Railway.

And what happened to the man who was largely responsible for bringing trains to the Grand Canyon? In 1898, O'Neill became mayor of Prescott, Arizona and quickly volunteered to serve in the Spanish-American War with Teddy Roosevelt and the Rough Riders. He was killed in action just before the charge up San Juan Hill. Today, you can ride the Grand Canyon Railway to the South Rim and stay in the Bucky O'Neill cabin at the Bright Angel Lodge.

The Kolb Brothers (Ellsworth and Emery)

In 1902, the two Kolb brothers bought out a Williams photography studio and set up shop on the South Rim of Grand Canyon to take photographs of the ever-increasing flow of tourists. Their first studio was a dirt-floor tent next to Ralph Cameron's hotel. They used a shallow mine shaft as a darkroom, and developed prints with murky water from cattle ponds far from the site. In 1904, they upgraded to a small frame studio on Cameron's mining claim at the Bright Angel Trailhead. With additions in 1915 and 1925, the Kolb Brothers' Lookout Studio today stands as one of the oldest buildings in Grand Canyon National Park. In 1905, Emery married, and in 1908, his daughter was the first European American child delivered (and for years the only European American child to live) at the Grand Canyon. In the winter of 1911–1912, the brothers made history by filming the first motion picture of a river run, which they showed at their studio and on numerous national lecture tours. The Kolb brothers earned a reputation as great photographers, expert guides, and geographers. Although Ellsworth eventually moved to Los Angeles, Emery stayed at the Grand Canyon for 73 years, until his death in 1976 at the age of 93. His was the longest recorded year-round residency at the canyon. He left behind tens of thousands of photographs and several hundred pieces of camera equipment that tell a fascinating story of the Grand Canyon experience.

LICENSED OUTFITTERS

GRAND CANYON COMMERCIAL BACKPACKERS, DAY HIKERS, BICYCLISTS

Company	Activity	Phone/Fax
Adventure Travel West Inc. P.O. Box 121 Idledale, CO 80453 info@at-west.com www.at-west.com	Hiking	303/697-6688 fax 303/697-5384
Adventures in Good Company 5913 Brackenridge Ave. Baltimore, MD 21212 www.adventuresingoodcompany.com	Backpacking (women only)	410/435-1965 877/439-4042 fax 410/435-3084
Angel's Gate Tours 112 Kletha Trail Flagstaff, AZ 86001 info@angelsgatetours.com www.angelsgatetours.com	Hiking Backpacking	928/856-1698 800/957-4557
Backroads 801 Cedar St. Berkeley, CA 94710 www.backroads.com	Bicycling	510/527-1555 800/462-2848 fax 510/527-1444
Boundless Journeys 1250 Waterbury Rd., Ste. 1 Stowe, VT 05672 info@boundlessjourneys.com www.boundlessjourneys.com	Hiking	802/253-1840 800/941-8010 fax 802/253-1844
Canyon Rim Adventures P.O. Box 304 Kanab, UT 84741 canyonrim@kanab.net www.canyonrimadventures.com	Bicycling Hiking	435/644-8512 800/897-9633
Discovery Treks 28248 N. Tatum Blvd. Cave Creek, AZ 85331 adventures@discoverytreks.com www.discoverytreks.com	Backpacking Hiking	480/247-9266 888/256-8731 fax 480/383-6321

Escape Adventures 8221 W. Charleston, #101 Las Vegas, NV 89117 info@escapeadventures.com www.escapeadventures.com	Cycling	702/596-2953 800/596-2953 fax 702/838-6968
Four Season Guides 107 West Phoenix Ave. Flagstaff, AZ 86001 www.fsguides.com	Hiking	928/525-1552
Grand Canyon Hikes 7010 Bader Rd. Flagstaff, AZ 86001 info@grandcanyonhikes.com www.grandcanyonhikes.com	Hiking Backpacking	928/779-1614 877/506-6233
High Sonoran Adventures 10628 N. 97 St. Scottsdale, AZ 85260 www.hikethecanyon.com	Backpacking Cycling	480/614-3331 877/472-6311
Just Roughin' It Adventure Company P.O. Box 1298 Chandler, AZ 85244-4298 info@justrouginit.com www.justroughinit.com	Backpacking Hiking	480/857-2477 877/399-2477 fax 480/857-2703
Northern Arizona University Outdoors P.O. Box 5773 Flagstaff, AZ 86011 www.nau.edu/outdoors	Backpacking	520/523-3229
Rim Tours 1233 S. Hwy. 191 Moab, UT 84532 www.rimtours.com	Mountain Biking	435/259-5223 800/626-7335
Sierra Club Outings Department 85 2nd St., 2nd Fl. San Francisco, CA 94105 national.outings@sierraclub.org www.sierraclub.org/outings	Backpacking	415/977-5522

Sky Island Treks 928 S. 7th Ave. Tucson, AZ 85701 backpacking@skyislandtreks.com www.skyislandtreks.com	Backpacking Hiking	520/622-6966
Telluride Academy P.O. Box 2255 Telluride, CO 81435 www.tellurideacademy.com	Backpacking	970/728-5311
The Wildland Trekking Company 3127 North Park Dr. Flagstaff, AZ 86004 www.wildlandtrekking.com	Day Hiking	800/715-4453
The World Outdoors 2840 Wilderness Pl., Ste. D Boulder, CO 80301 fun@theworldoutdoors.com www.theworldoutdoors.com	Hiking Bicycling	303/413-0938 800/488-8483 fax 303/413-0926
Timberline Adventures 7975 E. Harvard, Ste. J Denver, CO 80231 timber@earthnet.net www.timbertours.com	Day Hiking	303/368-4418 800/417-2453 fax 303/368-1651
Western Spirit Cycling 478 Mill Creek Rd. Moab, UT 84532 biking@westernspirit.com www.westernspirit.com	Mountain Biking Camping	435/259-8732 800/845-2453 fax 435/259-2736

WHITE-WATER RAFTING COMPANIES

Company	Phone/Fax
Aramark-Wilderness River Adventures P.O. Box 717 Page, AZ 86040 www.riveradventures.com	928/645-3296 800/992-8022 fax 928/645-6113
Arizona Raft Adventures, Inc. 4050 E. Huntington Dr. Flagstaff, AZ 86004 www.azraft.com	928/526-8200 800/786-7238 fax 928/526-8246

Arizona River Runners, Inc. 602/867-4866
P.O. Box 47788 800/477-7238
Phoenix, AZ 85068 fax 602/867-2174
www.raftarizona.com

Canyoneers, Inc. 928/526-0924
P.O. Box 2997 800/525-0924
Flagstaff, AZ 86004 fax 928/527-9398
www.canyoneers.com

Canyon Explorations, Inc. 928/774-4559
P.O. Box 310 800/654-0723
Flagstaff, AZ 86002 fax 928/774-4655
www.canyonexplorations.com

Colorado River & 801/261-1789
Trail Expeditions, Inc. 800/253-7328
P.O. Box 57575 fax 801/268-1193
Salt Lake City, UT 84157
www.crateinc.com

Diamond River Adventures, Inc. 928/645-8866
P.O. Box 1300 800/343-3121
Page, AZ 86040 fax 928/645-9536
www.diamondriver.com

Grand Canyon Discovery 928/526-8200
4050 E. Huntington Dr. 800/786-7238
Flagstaff, AZ 86004 fax 928/526-8246
www.grandcanyondiscovery.com

Grand Canyon Expeditions 435/644-2691
P.O. Box 0 800/544-2691
Kanab, UT 84741 fax 435/644-2699
www.gcex.com

Hatch River Expeditions, Inc. 928/355-2241
HC 67 Box 35 800/433-8966
Marble Canyon, AZ 86036 fax 928/355-2266
www.hatchriverexpeditions.com

Hualapai River Runners 928/769-2419
887 Route 66 fax 928/769-2637
Peach Springs, AZ 86434
www.grandcanyonresort.com
Note: Hualapai River Runners is not a National Park Service concessionaire
and is not regulated by the National Park Service.

Moki Mac River Expeditions, Inc.	801/268-6667
P.O. Box 71242	800/284-7280
Salt Lake City, UT 84171	fax 801/262-0935
www.mokimac.com	

OARS	209/736-4677
(Outdoor Adventure	800/346-6277
River Specialists)	fax 209/736-2902
P.O. Box 67	
Angels Camp, CA 95222	
www.oars.com	

Outdoors Unlimited	928/526-2852
6900 Townsend Winona Rd.	800/637-7238
Flagstaff, AZ 86004	fax 928/526-6185
www.outdoorsunlimited.com	

Tour West, Inc.	801/225-0755
P.O. Box 333	800/453-9107
Orem, UT 84059	fax 801/225-7979
www.twriver.com	

Western River Expeditions	801/942-6669
7258 Racquet Club Dr.	800/453-7450
Salt Lake City, UT 84121	fax 801/942-8514
www.westernriver.com	

PLACE NAMES OF THE GRAND CANYON

The Alligator: This low-lying ridge is named for its shape, which resembles the silhouette of an alligator.

Apache Point: Named for the Apache Indians of Arizona.

Asbestos Canyon: John Hance and William Ashurst discovered an asbestos vein here in the late 1800s.

Ayer Point: Located near Hance Canyon. Mrs. Edward E. Ayer was the first white woman to visit the Grand Canyon (1885) and travel down into the canyon via the Hance Trail.

Bass Camp: Named after local legend William Wallace Bass (1841–1933), who set up camp here during his search for trails into the canyon in 1884. He went on to build guesthouses, ferry crossings, and copper and asbestos mines in the canyon.

Bass Tomb: When Bass died in 1933, he left orders for his body to be cremated and his ashes scattered over Holy Grail Temple, or Bass Tomb.

Beale Point: Named for Lt. Edward Fitzgerald Beale, who in 1857–1858 was in charge of the survey party for a wagon road along the 35th Parallel. Beale used camels for pack animals.

Bedivere Point: Inspired by scenery that resembled places described in the Holy Grail legends, Richard T. Evans in 1902 named parts of the canyon after characters from Arthurian legends. Some places thus named include Bedivere Point, King Arthur Castle, Lancelot Point, Merlin Abyss, and Mordred Abyss.

Boucher Creek: Named in honor of Louis D. Boucher, who arrived at the Grand Canyon in 1891 and established one of the first tourist camps.

Boulder Creek: What else are you going to call a creek filled with boulders?

Boysag Point: This point, located at the North Rim, is accessible only by a small artificial bridge, hence the Piute word for bridge, *boysag*.

Brahma Temple: Fantastic natural formations gave rise to mystical names, like this corruption of the Hindu word for prayer or supreme creator of the Universe.

Breezy Point: When early residents Emery C. and Ellsworth Kolb stood at this point, the breeze was so strong it lifted gravel from the ground.

Bright Angel Creek: On August 16, 1869, after enduring four straight days of rain, mudslides, and flooding, the expedition party of Major John Wesley Powell came upon a peaceful, clear little creek he named "Bright Angel" (in contrast to the Dirty Devil River in Utah).

Buddha Temple: This feature of the canyon was so named because it resembles a Buddhist temple. This name was in use as early as 1900.

Burro Canyon: Thousands of wild burros used to flock to this canyon for water. It was also the name of a local Native American family.

Cape Final: In 1880, Major Clarence E. Dutton came to the end of a five-mile ride that left him at this spot gazing out over the canyon. Dutton said, "It is doubtless the most interesting spot on the Kaibab."

Cape Royal: This point was named by Major Clarence E. Dutton in 1882. In his words, it is a "congregation of wonderful structures, countless and vast, profound lateral chasms."

Cardenas Butte: García López de Cárdenas was a member of the Coronado expedition of 1540 that searched for the Seven Cities of Cibola. Sent to look for a "great canyon," he became the first white man known to have seen the Grand Canyon.

Chemehuevi Point: Named for Chemehuevi Indians, a branch of the Piute tribe.

Cheops Pyramid: Named for Cheops, the Egyptian pharaoh who built the Great Pyramid. George Wharton James says that Cheops Pyramid at the Grand Canyon has a "peculiar shape as of some quaint and Oriental device of symbolic significance."

Chuar Butte: Chuar is short for the name Chuarrumpeak, who was a young chief of the Kaibab Paiute tribe in the 1870s.

Cochise Butte: This butte was named for Cochise, chief of the Chircahua Apaches in the 1860s to early 1870s.

Colorado River: The name is said to come from a Spanish word meaning "red," probably because of the reddish color of the earth around the great river. As far as we know, it was first called this by a Spanish assistant to Father Kino in 1699.

Comanche Point: Originally called "Bissel Point" by George Wharton James in the late 1800s, it was later renamed by the U.S. Geographic Board in honor of the tribe of Plains Indians.

Confucius Temple: Confucius (551–478 B.C.) was the most famous sage of China. This natural formation is another instance of fanciful resemblance to temples associated with the prophets and founders of world religions.

Cope Butte: Edward Drinker Cope (1840–1897) was a noted American paleontologist. In the 1870s, he investigated the cretaceous and tertiary strata of the West.

Coronado Butte: In 1540, Francisco Vásquez de Coronado was the leader of a mission to explore the Southwest in search of the Seven Cities of Cibola, a mythical place of unlimited riches. He instead found the mud and stone Zuni villages. He returned to Mexico disheartened and empty-handed.

Cremation Creek: This creek lies at the bottom of Cremation Point (the second above Yavapai Point), where tribal legends speak of funeral cremations and the spreading of ashes over cliffs.

Crystal Creek: A creek with famously clear water, where the first pilots to fly into the Grand Canyon searched for a missing honeymooning couple who perished while boating through the canyon in 1927.

Dana Butte: This butte was named for U.S. geologist James Dwight Dana (1813–1895). Dana, a professor of geology at Yale University, wrote more than 200 scientific books and papers.

Darwin Plateau: This plateau was named for Charles Darwin, the evolutionist and British naturalist who proposed species changed through natural selection.

DeMotte Park: This open glade on the Kaibab Plateau was named by Major John Wesley Powell in August 1872, for his friend Dr. Harvey C. DeMotte, professor of mathematics at Wesleyan University and fellow expedition member.

Deubendorff Rapids: Deubendorff, a boatman for the 1909 Galloway-Stone Expedition, capsized in these rapids. The four-boat expedition ran from Green River, Wyoming to Needles, California in two months and one week, the fastest on record.

Devil's Corkscrew: This portion of the Bright Angel Trail is so named because it winds and twists downward for 1,200 feet.

Dunn Butte: William H. Dunn was a member of Major John Wesley Powell's first Colorado River expedition in 1869.

Dutton Point: Named for Major Clarence E. Dutton, a famous geologist and author of *The Tertiary History of the Grand Canyon District* (1882). Dutton was responsible for many place names in the Grand Canyon.

Elves Chasm: This chasm contains fantastic forms of travertine and wildflowers of columbine and orchids. A trip into this beautiful little canyon is like a visit to fairyland.

Escalante Creek: Named by Major John Wesley Powell in honor of the daring adventurer Father Silvestre Velez de Escalante, who crossed the Colorado River in the late 1700s.

Farview Point: Near Point Imperial. There is a broad view of the Painted Desert from this point.

Galloway Canyon: Nathaniel Galloway was a Mormon trapper who floated down the Colorado through the canyon on two expeditions around the turn of the century.

Garces Terrace: Named for Father Francisco Garces, who in 1775 made contact with the Havasupai and other tribes south of the Grand Canyon. In 1781, while serving as priest at the mission near what is now Yuma, he was killed by American Indians.

Garden Creek: At the lower end of this creek, Native Americans ran irrigation ditches for their gardens, hence the name.

Grand Canyon Village: This is the main tourist accommodation point and park administration area for the Grand Canyon.

Grandview Trail: The Grandview Trail was completed in 1893 by Pete Berry, who built the trail for access to his copper mine. The name, also used for the Grandview Hotel in 1904 and Grandview Caves in 1897, derives from the obvious: one heck of a view.

Granite Gorge: Large masses of pink and white granite give this 40-mile gorge its name. It covers river miles 77–118.

Great Thumb Point: So named because its shape resembles a large thumb from above.

Greenland Spring: This spring lies on what is known as the Greenland or Walhalla Plateau. Walhalla Plateau has been the official name since 1902, but before that, Mormon cattlemen referred to the plateau as Greenland.

Hakatai Canyon: Hakatai is the Havasupai name for the Colorado River, meaning "a large roaring sound."

Hance Creek: Hance Creek was named for John Hance (1839–1919), a legendary pioneer and resident of the South Rim in the late 1800s. He paved the way for visitors to see the canyon and spun wild tales of digging out the canyon himself and using the dirt to build the San Francisco Peaks.

Hancock Butte: Named after Captain William Augustus Hancock (1831–1902), surveyor, post trader, and sheriff in southern Arizona.

Hansbrough Point: Peter Hansbrough was an ill-fated member of the Robert Brewster Stanton expedition of 1889. He drowned after his boat capsized and was buried at the point that bears his name.

Havasu Canyon: The Havasupai Indians lived in and around the Grand Canyon. *Havasu* comes from the words *haha*, "water," and *vasu*, "blue," and translates as "blue water."

Hermit Basin: This area was named after Louis Boucher, "The Hermit," a reclusive French Canadian who established a camp to provide sleeping and eating accommodations for tourists who came down the trail to the Colorado River bed. His was the first provision for travelers near the river.

Hillers Butte: John K. Hillers was a photographer on the second Grand Canyon expedition under Major John Wesley Powell in 1871–1872.

Hindu Amphitheater: In 1882 Major Clarence E. Dutton wrote that this natural amphitheater was marked by its "profusion and richness [which] suggests an oriental character."

Hopi Point: This point was named for the Hopi Indians, who live on the Hopi Reservation. Their name is translated as the "Peaceful People."

Howlands Butte: Brothers Seneca and O. G. Howland were members of Major John Wesley Powell's first Grand Canyon expedition in 1869. After encountering the severity of the Colorado River rapids, they left the party, climbed up the canyon, and were killed by Native Americans on Shivwits Plateau.

Hualapai Canyon: The Hualapai Indians live today on a reservation south of the canyon. Some early histories describe them as a fierce tribe in the early territorial days of Arizona.

Hubbell Butte: Juan Lorenzo Hubbell (1853–1930) settled on the Navajo Indian Reservation at Ganado, Arizona in 1871 as a pioneer trader. He also served as county sheriff and in the state senate.

Imperial Point (Point Imperial): This is the highest point along either rim of the Grand Canyon. Its lofty status may have inspired the name "imperial."

Indian Garden: According to George Wharton James, this spot had been cultivated by a Havasupai family years before white men set eyes on it. It is today a resting point for those who make the descent into the canyon along Bright Angel Trail.

Isis Temple: George Wharton James said that this temple-like formation was named for the goddess of the Egyptians and that in front of it are two notable great cloisters.

Ives Point: Lieutenant Joseph Christmas Ives was the first military man to explore the Colorado River to its headwaters for navigational purposes. In 1851 he made a surveying trip from west to east across Arizona.

Johnson Point: Fred Johnson was a Grand Canyon National Park ranger who drowned in 1929 at Horn Creek Rapid while performing official duties.

Kaibab Plateau: In 1874, Major John Wesley Powell noted that the great plateau forming the North Rim of the Grand Canyon was called by the Native Americans Kai-vav-wi, "a mountain lying down." In English this became Kaibab Plateau. The Paiutes refer to the great forests lying on this plateau as the Kaibabits.

Kanab Canyon: From the Paiute word for "willow." Kanab Canyon was where the exhausted Powell expedition received sorely needed rations from team packers Joe Hamblin, George Adair, and Nathan Adams, who had traveled down the canyon and waited for the explorers.

Kanab Creek: Many willow trees along this creek gave it its name.

Kolb (Natural) Bridge: Named for Emery C. Kolb, who, with his brother Ellsworth, became famous for his photographs and explorations of the Grand Canyon. The name was suggested by Senator Barry Goldwater.

Kwagunt Valley: In 1869, this valley was named by Major John Wesley Powell after a Paiute Indian named Quagunt (or Kwagunt), who was very friendly to the exploring party. The Paiute Indians said that Quagunt owned the valley, which was a gift from his father.

Lava Falls: The Powell expedition of 1871 observed that the canyon appeared to have once been filled with lava to a depth of 1,500 feet. They named the descent Lava Falls.

Lipan Point: The first mention of the Lipan Indians occurred in 1699, when they were named as allies of the Comanches. In 1902, the name of this point was changed from Lincoln to Lipan.

Lyell Butte: Sir Charles Lyell (1798–1875) was a British geologist whose noted work, *The Principles of Geology,* published in 1830 and 1832, was a direct forerunner of the theory of evolution advanced by Charles Darwin.

Manzanita Point: This point was named by Colonel John White, a canyon resident in the 1920s. On one visit to the North Rim, he ascended Bright Angel Creek and noticed a large manzanita bush. There he wrote on a piece of wood, "Manzanita Point."

Marble Gorge: On August 9, 1869, Major John Wesley Powell wrote that his exploring party passed between cliffs of marble in which were a great number of caves. He named the gorge Marble Canyon.

Maricopa Point: This point was named to honor the Maricopa Indians, a tribe living in south-central Arizona, noted for friendliness to white settlers.

Marsh Butte: George Wharton James named this place for the U.S. paleontologist Othniel Charles Marsh (1831–1899). Marsh investigated fossils of the western United States, among them the early ancestors of horses.

Matkatamiba Canyon: Matkatamiba is the name of an old Havasupai Indian family.

Matthes Point: In 1902, Francois E. Matthes was in charge of making the first topographic map of the Grand Canyon. He was responsible for many of the names based on mythological deities following Clarence Dutton's lead.

Mohave Point: The Mohave Indians lived along the Colorado River. Their name, meaning "three mountains," came from the fact that the tribe lived near the Needles, a group of three sharp peaks located in Mohave County, Arizona. The town of Needles was relocated across the river in California.

Monument Creek: A single shaft, about 100 feet high and resembling a great monument, is visible from the rim at this point.

Moran Point: Thomas Moran was an artist who first visited the North Rim in 1873 with Major John Wesley Powell. Although his paintings of the Grand Canyon were largely responsible for making the U.S. public aware of the wonders of the Grand Canyon, the point is actually named for his brother Peter who accompanied the Bourke 1881 expedition as an artist.

Mount Hayden: Charles Trumbull Hayden came to Arizona in 1857 on the first Butterfield Overland Stage. In 1870, he established Hayden's Ferry, now called Tempe.

Muav Canyon: This canyon was probably named after a Paiute word meaning "divide" or "pass" because of the presence of the Muav Saddle, a pass in the canyon rim at the top of the north wall. Powell spoke of it by this name in 1869.

Nankoweap Butte: The word means "place where Indians had a fight," which is apparently what happened here at some point in canyon history (an Apache attack on Kaibab Paiute).

Neal Spring: This spring at the head of Bright Angel Canyon was named for a local cowpuncher.

140-Mile Canyon: The Powell Grand Canyon expeditions named several canyons according to their distance from the party's entrance to the Grand Canyon.

O'Neill Spring: This spring on Horseshoe Mesa was named for Jim O'Neill, a scout for General George Crook.

Osiris Temple: Another one of the fancifully named features, this one for the chief deity of the ancient Egyptian pantheon.

Paiute Point: A lookout named for the Paiute Indians, the tribe native to the area north of the Grand Canyon.

Palisades of the Desert: These bold cliffs are at the western border of the Painted Desert. The name was proposed by Francois E. Matthes in 1902.

Papago Point: This point was named for the Papago tribe of southern and southwestern Arizona and northern Sonora.

Paya Point: This point was named for Lemuel Paya, a Havasupai Indian, once a member of the Supai Tribal Council.

Phantom Ranch: The Phantom Ranch is the only area at the bottom of the Grand Canyon with guest accommodations. Once called Rust Camp, it was renamed by Mary Colter for its haze that creates an illusory effect on the narrow gorge.

Pima Point: A lookout named for the Pima Indians, a peaceful, agricultural tribe living in south-central Arizona.

Point Sublime: Major Clarence E. Dutton spent many hours on this point, writing descriptions of Grand Canyon scenery. He is said to have called it "the most sublime of the earthly spectacles." He named the promontory in 1880.

Powell Plateau: In 1869, Major John Wesley Powell led the first successful Euro-American exploration of the canyon's towering walls and dangerous rapids and named it the Grand Canyon. In 1871–1872, Powell again explored the canyon, making scientific records. Powell later became the first director of the U.S. Geological Survey and of the U.S. Bureau of American Ethnology. A monument at Powell Point (Powell Point Memorial) commemorates his achievements in the Grand Canyon. The plateau was named in 1882 by Clarence Dutton.

Putesoi Canyon: Putesoi is the name of a Havasupai Indian family.

Ribbon Falls: Beneath the North Rim, this single fall drops down in a cut from an overhang and makes a moss-green, ribbonlike track against the red wall of the canyon.

Roaring Springs: These springs at the head of Bright Angel Creek gush with such force from the canyon wall that they make a true roaring sound. The water then plunges 400 feet down a fern-covered slope.

Rowe Well: In June 1890, Sanford Rowe, a pioneer stockman and guide, began digging here in search of underground water. He later developed Rowe Well into an auto camp.

Santa Maria Spring: This spring, about 1,760 feet below Hermit Trailhead, was named by Mary Colter, the architect for many of the South Rim buildings.

Sapphire Canyon: Major John Wesley Powell named this canyon for its coloring.

Shinumo Altar: Named by Frederick Dellenbaugh, who thought the 600-foot formation resembled a great altar. Shinumo comes from the Paiute Indian name for the area's earliest residents.

Shiva Temple: Shiva Temple is a wooded butte that was once part of the North Rim. It was named after a Hindu god by Major Clarence E. Dutton in 1880. He described it as "the grandest of all the buttes, and the most majestic in aspect, though not the most ornate."

Shoshone Point: Named for the Shoshone Indian tribe of northwest Wyoming.

Sinking Ship: The tilting of the strata in this formation gives it the appearance of a sinking ship.

Sinyala Canyon: George Wharton James's favored guide was a Havasupai named Sinyala.

60-Mile Creek: This creek is about 60 miles below Lees Ferry. Apparently this name was suggested by Francois E. Matthes, Richard F. Evans, and J. R. Evans.

Sockdolager Rapids: Sockdolager is 1800s British and American slang for a "heavy or knock-down blow" or a "finisher." It is the word chosen by Powell's expedition team to describe a particularly awesome set of rapids that had them shaking in their boots.

Stanton Point: This point was named by Robert Brewster Stanton (1846–1922), who headed an 1890 boat expedition down the Colorado River in Grand Canyon to study the feasibility of a railroad along the canyon floor.

Sturdevant Point: Glen E. Sturdevant was a park naturalist who drowned in the Colorado River just below this point in 1929.

Supai: This is the official name for the Havasupai village that is the center of tribal activities. A "Supai" reservation was created on June 8, 1880, but the area later underwent changes, with the present 518 acres being set aside on March 31, 1882, for the "Yavai Suppai" Indians. This village is subject to severe floods. In 1910, a rim-to-rim, 40-foot wall of water swept away all buildings while the residents clung to the cliff sides and watched the raging torrent. Today, an estimated 235 Havasupai live on the reservation. The tribe also has rights to 2,540 acres in Cataract Canyon.

Tanner Canyon: In 1889, Seth B. Tanner helped build a trail from the South Rim down into the canyon to the Colorado River, to reach his mining claims.

Thor's Hammer: George Wharton James said that he named this formation because of its resemblance to a hammer huge enough to be used by the Norse god Thor.

Tilted Mesa: Francois E. Matthes suggested this name for the sloping tableland west of Marble Gorge, on the Kaibab Monocline.

Toltec Point: The name derives from an archaeological theory, which posited that Toltec Indians from Mexico had contacts as far north as the Gila River in Arizona.

Tonto Trail: This trail is on the South Rim on the Tonto Platform. It was named for the so-called Tonto Apaches, a term that included members of several tribes.

Tovar Terrace: Named after Pedro de Tobar (or Tovar), an aristocratic member of the 1540 Coronado expedition, who learned of the Grand Canyon in his conversations with Hopi Indians. When he reported this to Coronado, Cárdenas was sent to investigate.

Tower of Ra: In ancient Egyptian mythology, Ra was the god of the sun, a principal deity. The pharaohs claimed to be Ra's incarnations.

Tower of Set: Set was the Egyptian god of war. This location was named by the artist Thomas Moran in 1879.

The Transept: Major Clarence E. Dutton wrote in 1882 that this portion of the Grand Canyon's North Rim is "the finest and most picturesque of the gorges of the Kaibab front...far grander than Yosemite."

Travertine Canyon: Waters heavily charged with calcium carbonate leave a deposit of smooth, soft green stone called travertine. Seepage has deposited travertine all over this canyon wall. There are actually two such canyons, at river miles 95.5 and 229.

Tusayan Ruin: This small ruin, once inhabited by pueblo dwellers around A.D. 1200, lies behind the Tusayan Museum on the South Rim of the Grand Canyon. Spaniards used the name Tusayan for the Hopi mesas and villages.

Upset Rapids: In 1923, the USGS Birdseye expedition mapping the Grand Canyon had its first boat upset in this hitherto-unnamed location.

Vasey's Paradise: George W. Vasey (1822–1893) served as a botanist with the U.S. Department of Agriculture 1872–1893. He was a valuable member of Powell's expedition to the Rocky Mountains in 1868.

Vishnu Temple: The Hindu god Vishnu is a member of the supreme trinity, along with Brahman and Shiva. The butte was named in 1880 by Major Clarence E. Dutton.

Vista Encantadora: In 1941, the original name of Vista Encantada ("enchanted view") was boldly changed by Park Supervisor Dr. Harold C. Bryant to Vista Encantadora ("enchanting view") to be grammatically correct.

Watahomigi Point: This point is located on the South Rim, a few miles south of Havasu Falls. It was named for a Havasupai Indian family.

Wescogame Point: This point was named for a Havasupai Indian family whose members still live nearby.

Widforss Point: In December 1937, this point was named to honor Gunnar Mauritz Widforss, an artist whose canyon paintings remain some of the best ever done. He died on the canyon rim in 1943.

Yaki Point: This point was named just prior to 1910, when the Yaqui Indians of Mexico were struggling with the Mexican government against being transported from their home in northern Mexico. Many Yaquis fled to the United States for refuge.

Yavapai Point: Named for the Yavapai Indians of Arizona, actually Apache–Mohave who lived along Arizona's Verde River.

Yuma Point: The Yuma Indians inhabit the lower reaches of the Colorado River where Yuma, Arizona, is today.

Zoroaster Temple: Named after Zoroaster, the founder of the ancient national religion of the Perso-Iranian people. Both G. W. James and Clarence Dutton used this name for this formation.

Zuni Point: This point was named for a tribe of Native Americans that lives in New Mexico near the Arizona border, northeast of Springerville. The "Seven Cities of Cibola" were thought by the Spanish to be in the Zuni homeland.

Partially excerpted from *Grand Canyon Place Names,* by Byrd H. Granger (University of Arizona Press, 1999).

TELEPHONE AND WEBSITE DIRECTORY

GETTING THERE

AMTRAK Corporation	800/872-7245
Current road conditions (24-hour)	928/638-7888
Educational fee waivers	928/638-7850
Flagstaff Express Shuttle	928/225-2290 or 800/563-1980
Grand Canyon Airport	928/638-2446
Grand Canyon Railway www.thetrain.com	800/843-8724
Greyhound Bus Line	928/774-4573 (Flagstaff office) or 800/231-2222
National Park Service Grand Canyon information	928/638-7888
Open Road Tours	928/226-8060 or 877/226-8060
Transportation Desk: North Rim	928/638-2612
Transportation Desk: South Rim	928/638-2631

PARK ATTRACTIONS

Backcountry Office: South Rim	928/638-7875
Canyon View Information Plaza	928/638-7644
Desert View Information Station	928/638-7893
Havasupai Tourist Enterprise www.havasupaitribe.com	928/448-2121, 928/448-2141, 928/448-2174, or 928/448-2180
Kolb Studio	928/638-2771
North Rim Visitor Center	928/638-7864
Tusayan Ruin & Museum	928/638-2305
Yavapai Observation Station	928/638-2631

GETTING AROUND

Current road conditions (24-hour)	928/638-7888
Grand Canyon Field Institute study trips www.grandcanyon.org/fieldinstitute	928/638-2485 or 866/471-4435

Grand Canyon Motorcoach Tours through Xanterra www.grandcanyonlodges.com	303/297-2757 or 888/297-2757
Grand Canyon Railway www.thetrain.com	800/843-8724
Grand Canyon Taxi	928/638-2822 or 928/638-2631, ext. 6563
North Kaibab Ranger Station (North Rim)	928/643-7395
Trans-Canyon Shuttle	928/638-2820
Tusayan Ranger Station (South Rim)	928/638-2443

Air Tours

Air Grand Canyon Family Tours www.airgrandcanyon.com	928/638-2686 or 800/247-4726
Grand Canyon Helicopters www.grandcanyonhelicoptersaz.com	928/638-2764 or 800/541-4537
Maverick Helicopters www.maverickhelicopter.com	702/261-0007 or 888/261-4414
Papillon Grand Canyon Helicopters www.papillon.com	928/638-2419 or 800/528-2418
Sundance Helicopters www.helicoptour.com	

LODGING AND DINING
Grand Canyon National Park Lodges
(Xanterra Parks and Resorts)

Advance reservations www.grandcanyonlodges.com	303/297-2757 or 888/297-2757 928/638-2631 (Same-day reservations)

Other

Grand Canyon Kennels	928/638-0534
Grand Canyon Music Festival www.grandcanyonmusicfest.org	928/638-9215 or 800/997-8285

CAMPING AND BACKPACKING
Camping Reservations Inside Park

Backcountry Information Center	928/638-7875
Mather Campground (South Rim) www.recreation.gov	877/444-6777
North Rim Campground www.recreation.gov	877/444-6777
Trailer Village (South Rim) www.grandcanyonlodges.com	303/297-2757 or 888/297-2757 928/638-2631 (same-day reservations)

Camping Outside Park

Camper Village (Tusayan)	928/638-2887
DeMotte Campground (North Rim)	928/643-7395
Jacob Lake Campground (North Rim)	928/643-7395
Kaibab Camper Village (North Rim)	928/643-7804 summer, 928/526-0924 winter
Kaibab National Forest (North Rim)	928/635-8200
Kaibab National Forest (South Rim)	928/638-2443
Ten-X Campground	928/638-2443
Tuweep Ranger Station	928/716-2843

RECREATIONAL OPPORTUNITIES
Mule and Horseback Riding

Apache Stables (horseback trail rides outside park, South Rim) www.apachestables.com	928/638-2891 or 928/638-3105
Canyon Trail Rides (mule trips, North Rim) www.canyonrides.com	435/679-8665
Hualapai Hilltop (Western Grand Canyon) www.havasupaitribe.com	928/448-2121, 928/448-2141, 928/448-2174, or 928/448-2180
Xanterra (mule trips, South Rim) www.grandcanyonlodges.com	303/297-2757 or 888/297-2757

River Trips

Raft the Canyon (smooth-water trips) www.raftthecanyon.com	888/522-6644

Fishing

Lees Ferry Anglers (Lees Ferry) www.leesferry.com	928/355-2261 or 800/962-9755
Marble Canyon Lodge (Lees Ferry) www.lessferryflyfishing.com	928/645-9235 or 800/533-7339
Xanterra (Phantom Ranch) www.grandcanyonlodges.com	303/297-2757 or 888/297-2757

Bicycle Shops

Absolute Bikes www.absolutebikes.net	928/779-5969 (Flagstaff), 928/284-1242 (Sedona)
Cosmic Cycles (Flagstaff)	928/779-1092
Mountain Bike Heaven (Sedona) www.mountainbikeheaven.com	928/282-1312
Sedona Bike & Bean (Sedona) www.bike-bean.com	928/284-0210
Sedona Sports (Sedona) www.sedonasports.com	928/282-1317

Winter Activities

North Kaibab Ranger Station (North Rim)	928/643-7395
Tusayan Ranger Station (South Rim)	928/638-2443

AMERICAN INDIAN RESERVATIONS

Havasupai Tourist Enterprise www.havasupaitribe.com	928/448-2121, 928/448-2141, 928/448-2174, or 928/448-2180
Hopi Cultural Center	928/734-2401
Hualapai Tribal Enterprises	928/769-2419
Kaibab Paiute Cultural Office	928/643-6014
Navajo Nation Parks and Recreation	928/871-6645

AREA ATTRACTIONS

Arboretum at Flagstaff www.thearb.org	928/774-1442
Canyon de Chelly National Monument www.nps.gov/cach	928/674-5500

Glen Canyon National Recreation Area www.glencanyonnha.org	928/608-6072
Grand Canyon Skywalk www.grandcanyonskywalk.com	702/878-9378 or 877/716-9378
Lowell Observatory, Flagstaff www.lowell.edu	928/774-3358
Meteor Crater www.meteorcrater.com	928/289-5898 or 800/289-5898
Montezuma Castle National Monument www.nps.gov/moca	928/567-3322
Monument Valley Navajo Tribal Park www.navajonationparks.org	928/672-2366
Museum of Northern Arizona, Flagstaff www.musnaz.org	928/774-5213
Sunset Crater National Monument www.nps.gov/sucr	928/556-7134
Tuzigoot Ruin National Monument www.nps.gov/tuzi	928/634-5564
Walnut Canyon National Monument www.nps.gov/waca	928/526-3367
Wupatki National Monument www.nps.gov/wupa	928/679-2365

ENVIRONMENTAL EDUCATION AND PRESERVATION

Arizona Game and Fish Department www.azgfd.gov	520/774-5045
Grand Canyon Association www.grandcanyon.org	928/638-2481 or 800/858-2808
Grand Canyon Field Institute www.grandcanyon.org/fieldinstitute	928/638-2485 or 866/471-4435
Grand Canyon National Park Foundation www.grandcanyonfoundation.org	928/774-1760
Grand Canyon Trust www.grandcanyontrust.org	928/774-7488 or 888/GCT-5550

NPS Environmental Education Programs www.nps.gov/archive/grca/education.	928/638-7762
Peregrine Fund www.peregrinefund.org	208/362-3716

VISITOR SERVICES IN SURROUNDING AREA

Flagstaff, Arizona (Chamber of Commerce) www.flagstaffchamber.com	928/774-4504
Flagstaff Visitor Center www.flagstaffarizona.org	928/774-9541
Kanab, Utah (Chamber of Commerce) www.kanabchamber.com	800/733-5263
Page-Lake Powell, Arizona (Chamber of Commerce) www.pagelakepowellchamber.org	928/645-2741 or 888/261-7243
Sedona, Arizona (Chamber of Commerce) www.sedonachamber.com	928/282-7722
Tusayan, Arizona (Chamber of Commerce) www.grandcanyonchamber.org	888/472-2696
Williams, Arizona (Chamber of Commerce) www.williamschamber.com	800/863-0546

WHERE CAN WE FIND...?

Where can we find a gas station?

Grand Canyon Chevron operates one service station on the South Rim at Desert View, located 25 miles east of the Village. Desert View Chevron is open 9 A.M.–5 P.M., with 24-hour gas and diesel available with a credit card. Outside the Park you will find a Conoco Gas Station (928/638-2608) in Tusayan, seven miles south of the Village.

On the North Rim, Grand Canyon Chevron (gasoline and propane fuels, no diesel) operates a service station on the North Rim Campground access road. Hours are daily 7 A.M.–7 P.M. in the winter season. The nearest diesel fuel is 18 miles north at the North Rim Country Store at the Kaibab Lodge.

Where can we find towing and repair services?

The Grand Canyon Garage operates a repair and towing facility located next door to the Grand Canyon National Park Lodges General Office building in Grand Canyon Village on the South Rim. It's open year-round daily 8 A.M.–noon and 1–5 P.M. Call Xanterra South Rim (928/638-2631) for 24-hour emergency vehicle towing. On the North Rim, the Grand Canyon Chevron station provides minor repairs (tires, etc.). The service station at Jacob Lake, 45 miles north, provides emergency repairs such as tires, belts, batteries, fuses, hoses, etc. Diesel fuel is not available at Jacob Lake.

Where can we find public restrooms? Showers? Laundromats?

There are public restrooms at all of the visitor and information centers and inside all lodging facilities throughout the park. On the South Rim, coin-operated shower and laundry facilities are located at the entrance to Mather Campground (daily 6 A.M.–11 P.M. with last load in at 9:45 P.M.—hours may vary in the winter). On the North Rim, you'll find coin-operated laundry and shower facilities on the access road leading to the North Rim Campground (May 15–October 15 daily 7 A.M.–10 P.M.).

Where can we find a post office?

The main post office (928/638-2512) at the Grand Canyon is located in Grand Canyon Village, across from the visitor center. It offers year-round window service Monday–Friday 9 A.M.–4:30 P.M., Saturday 11 A.M.–1 P.M. It's closed holidays, but stamps are available from a machine in the lobby, which is open 5 A.M.–10 P.M. On the North Rim the post office is located in the Grand Canyon Lodge complex with window service Monday–Friday 8 A.M.–noon and 1–5 P.M.

Where can we find a bank, cash a check, or exchange foreign currency?

There is a full-service Chase Bank (928/638-2437) in Market Plaza at Grand Canyon Village. Hours are Monday–Thursday 9 A.M.–5 P.M., and Friday 9 A.M.–6 P.M. It's closed weekends and holidays. The bank will cash travelers checks (including foreign travelers checks) and give cash advances on credit cards, but does not exchange foreign currency. A 24-hour ATM machine is available. There are banks in the gateway communities of Williams and Flagstaff, Arizona. The closest bank to the North Rim is located in Kanab, Utah. You can also cash travelers checks (if you're a hotel guest) at the front desks of most park lodges.

Where is the lost and found?

You can turn in or trace lost and found articles at the Visitor Center at Canyon View Information Plaza. Call Xanterra South Rim (928/638-2631) to report items lost or found in lodges, restaurants, or lounges on the South Rim. On the North Rim, call the NPS Visitor Center information desk or the Grand Canyon Lodge front desk. Or, if you wish to leave a report in person, contact the Grand Canyon National Park Lost and Found Office (Grand Canyon National Park, P.O. Box 129, Grand Canyon, AZ, 86023, 928/638-7798). When reporting the item, be sure to include your name, mailing address, phone number, description of the item you lost, where and when you lost it.

Where can we receive medical services?

Dial 911 (9-911 from hotel rooms) for 24-hour emergency fire, medical, or ranger assistance or to report accidents or injuries. On the South Rim, the North Country Community Health Center (928/638-2551) is open year-round 8 A.M.–6 P.M. with reduced hours mid-October–mid-May. On the North Rim, emergency medical services are provided by the rangers on duty.

Where can we get an America the Beautiful pass?

America the Beautiful—National Parks and Federal Recreational Lands Passes (good for all national parks for one year from the date of purchase) replaces the Golden Eagle Passport, National Parks Pass, and Golden Eagle Hologram pass. It can be purchased from rangers at park entrance stations, by phone (888/ASK-USGS ext. 1), or online (http://store.usgs.gov/pass). The cost is $80 annually. Golden Age Passes, which are lifetime passes to all national parks, have been replaced by the America the Beautiful—Senior Pass, which can also only be purchased at the same locations and require a one-time $10 fee when issued to qualifying senior citizens (U.S. citizens or legal residents age 62 or older).

Where can we find the Grand Canyon Field Institute office?

The Institute (928/638-2485 or 866/471-4435, gcfi@grandcanyon.org, www.grandcanyon.org/fieldinstitute) is headquartered at 4 Tonto Street in Grand Canyon Village, open Monday–Friday 8 A.M.–5 P.M.

Where can we find the Grand Canyon Association office?

The GCA (928/638-2481, www.grandcanyon.org) is headquartered in a building located at 1 Tonto Street in Grand Canyon Village.

Where can we find out about special visitor services?

The Grand Canyon National Park Accessibility Guide, indicating the accessibility of most public buildings, park facilities, and trails to visitors with disabilities, is available free upon request at NPS visitor and information centers, or you can download a PDF at www.nps.gov/grca/planyourvisit/accessibility.htm. The National Park Service provides wheelchairs for temporary day use by park visitors. No rental fee is charged. Wheelchairs are usually available on the South Rim at Canyon View Information Plaza and on the North Rim at the Visitor Center and Grand Canyon Lodge.

To obtain a temporary parking permit for designated parking, inquire at the Entrance Gates, Canyon View Information Plaza, or North Rim Visitor Center. Most shuttles are inaccessible to wheelchairs. Accessible shuttle buses are available in response to requests made at least 24 hours in advance. Call 928/638-0591.

Where can we find child day care?

Make sure you have your kids' immunization records with you when you drop them off at the Kaibab Learning Center (928/638-6333, Mon.–Fri. 7:30 A.M.–5:30 P.M.). Day care for infants to 12-year-olds is possible if space is available.

· Further Reading ·

The Ace in the Hole: A Brief History of Company 818 of the Civilian Conservation Corps by Louis Lester Purvis. Brentwood Christian Press, 1989.

Arizona Road and Recreation Atlas. Benchmark Maps, 1996.

Arizona, the Grand Canyon State by Steven L. Walker. Camelback, 1991.

Bibliography of the Grand Canyon and the Lower Colorado River from 1540 compiled by Earle E. Spamer. Grand Canyon Association, 1990.

Carving Grand Canyon: Evidence, Theories and Mystery by Wayne Ranney. Grand Canyon Association, 2005.

Checklist of the Birds, Mammals, Plants, Reptiles & Amphibians of the Grand Canyon Area compiled by Kathy Butterfield et al. Grand Canyon Association, 1993.

Colorado River in Grand Canyon: A Comprehensive Guide to Its Natural and Human History by Larry Stevens. Fifth edition. Red Lake Books, 1998.

The Exploration of the Colorado River and Its Canyons by John Wesley Powell. Dover, 1961.

Exploring the Grand Canyon: Adventures of Yesterday and Today by Lynne Foster. Grand Canyon Association, 1990.

A Field Guide to the Grand Canyon by Stephen Whitney. Second edition. Mountaineers Books, 1996.

Grand Canyon: A Different View by Tom Vail. Master Books, 2003

Grand Canyon Loop Hikes II by George Steck. Chockstone Press, 1993.

Grand Canyon National Park Road Guide by Jeremy Schmidt. Revised edition. Free Wheeling Travel Guides, 1997.

Grand Canyon Place Names by Byrd H. Granger. University of Arizona Press, 1999.

Grand Canyon, The Complete Guide by James Kaiser. Destination Press, 2007.

Grand Canyon Wildflowers by Arthur M. Phillips III. Grand Canyon Association, 1996.

Grand Canyon Women: Lives Shaped by Landscape by Betty Leavengood. Grand Canyon Association, 2004.

A Guide to Grand Canyon National Park and Vicinity by Sandra Scott. Grand Canyon Association, 1997.

A Guide to the Grand Canyon Village by Timothy Manns. Grand Canyon Association, 1996.

Havasuw 'Baaja: People of the Blue Green Water by Stephen Hirst. Havasupai Tribe, 1985.

The Hidden Canyon: A River Journey by John Blaustein. Chronicle Books, 1999.

Hikernut's Grand Canyon Companion by Lane and Kathleen Bryant. A Sense of Nature, 2007.

Hiking Grand Canyon National Park by Ron Adkinson. Second edition. Falcon, 2006.

Hiking the Grand Canyon (Sierra Club Totebook) by John Annerino. Sierra Club, 2006.

I Am the Grand Canyon: The Story of the Havasupai People by Stephen Hirst. Grand Canyon Association, 2007.

In the House of Stone and Light: An Introduction to the Human History of Grand Canyon by J. Donald Hughes. Grand Canyon Association, 1993.

An Introduction to Grand Canyon Ecology by Rose Houk. Grand Canyon Association, 1996.

An Introduction to Grand Canyon Geology by L. Greer Price. Grand Canyon Association, 1999.

Kaibab National Forest Maps. U.S. Forest Service, 1994.

Living At The Edge: Explorers, Exploiters and Settlers of the Grand Canyon Region by Michael F. Anderson. Grand Canyon Association, 1998.

The Majesty of the Grand Canyon: 150 Years in Art by Joni Louise Kinsey. First Glance Books, 1998.

Mammals of Grand Canyon by Donald F. Hoffmeister. University of Illinois, 1971.

Mary Colter: Builder Upon the Red Earth by Virginia Grattan. Revised edition. Grand Canyon Association, 1992.

Obsession: Harvey Butchart and the Exploration of the Grand Canyon by Elias Butler. Puma Press, 2007.

Official Guide to Hiking the Grand Canyon by Scott Thybony. Revised edition. Grand Canyon Association, 1997.

On the Edge of Splendor by Douglas W. Schwartz. School of American Research, 1989.

101 Questions About Desert Life by Alice Jablonsky. Southwest Parks and Monuments Association, 1994.

Plateau Journal: Land and Peoples of the Colorado Plateau. The Museum of Northern Arizona and the Grand Canyon Association, 1998.

Quest for the Pillar of Gold: The Mines and Miners of the Grand Canyon by George H. Billingsley and Earle E. Spamer. Grand Canyon Association, 1997.

River and Desert Plants of the Grand Canyon by Kristin Huisinga, Lori Makarick, Kate Watters, and Ann Zwinger. Mountain Press Publishing Company, 2006.

River Runners of the Grand Canyon by David Lavender. Grand Canyon Association, 1990.

River to Rim by Nancy Brian. Earthquest Press, 1992.

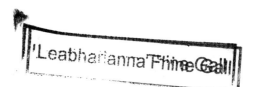

·Index·

D

daycare: *see* childcare services
Dead Horse Point State Park: 28
deer mice: 124
Delaware North Park Services: 14
Delicatessen at the Marketplace: 100
Deli in the Pines: 100
DeMotte Campground: 110–111
dental services: 77
Denver, Colorado, distance from: 3
desert bighorn sheep: 26, 39, 40, 41
Desert View: 75
Desert View, Arizona: 4, 170
Desert View Campground: 17, 109
Desert View Drive: 20, 74
Desert View Information Station: 20, 24
Desert View Point: 80
Desert View Trading Post: 11, 12, 99
Desert View Watchtower: 55, 170, 181
desert wood rat: 39
Deubendorff, Seymour S.: 167
digital photography: 87
dining: *see* food/restaurants
disabled visitors: 7, 72–73, 206
discounts: 177
Douglas firs: 51
Doyle Peak: 54
drinking water: 130–131
Dripping Springs: 164
driving distances: 2–3

E

eagles: 46, 47
East Rim Drive: *see* Desert View Drive
easy hikes: 134–135
Echo Cliffs: 26, 76
educational fee waivers: 7
educational programs and exhibits:
    173–175, 202–203
Egloffstein, F. W. von: 161
elk: 39
El Tovar Hotel: food/restaurants 11, 99;
    historical background 63, 166; lodging
    17, 90–91; Mary Colter 181; self-guided
    walking tours 84
emergency services: 205

entrance fees: 7
entrance points: 4–6
Environmental Education Programs:
    174–175, 203
erosion: 30, 31
Euro-American exploration and settle-
    ment: 60–61, 159–162

F

facts: 28, 145
falcons: 38, 46, 47
fall visits: fall foliage 54; hiking 132–133;
    weather conditions 8–9, 16
family attractions: 176–177
fauna: *see* animal population
feeding animals: 41–43, 124–125
field seminars: 71, 116
first-aid kits: 16, 131
fish/fishing: 38, 129, 148–149
Flagstaff and Grand Canyon Railroad
    Company: 163
Flagstaff, Arizona: airports 5; area attrac-
    tions 156; bus service 5–6; driving
    distances 2; food/restaurants 103–104;
    lodging 97–98; train service 163
flash floods: 9, 10, 122, 172
flashlights: 131
flora: *see* plants
food/restaurants: animal-proof food
    containers 124; Inner Canyon 100;
    North Rim 12, 100, 104; outside
    Grand Canyon 101–104; within Grand
    Canyon 99–100; South Rim 11, 99–100,
    101–104
Four Corners region: 27
Fredonia, Arizona: 6, 88
free shuttles: 20; *see also* shuttle services
frogs: 38
fur trade: 60, 160
future plans: 152

G

Galloway, Nathaniel: 167
Gallup, New Mexico, distance from: 2
Garces, Francisco Thomas: 60, 160
gas stations: 12, 204

Sonoran gopher snake: 38, 40–41
southern plateau lizard: 41
South Kaibab Trail: car travel 75; hiking tips 86; historical background 64; moderate hikes 137; ranger-led walks 114; shuttle services 68, 72; sightseeing tips 21; strenuous hikes 139
South Rim: access points 4–6; archaeological sites 57–58; backcountry regions 118; birds 46–47; campgrounds 108–109, 110; car travel 75; easy hikes 135; entrance points 4–5; food/restaurants 99–100, 101–104; hiking 21; horseback riding 146; itinerary tips 78–79; lodging 90–92, 94–98; moderate hikes 137; mule trips 82–83; night-time activities 34; plants 50–53; self-guided walking tours 84; shuttle services 72–73; sightseeing tips 20; strenuous hikes 139; sunrises/sunsets 35; transportation options 68–71; visitor services 11–12, 23–24; weather conditions 8, 16; wildflowers 50, 52; winter visits 88, 150
souvenirs: 66
Spanish exploration: 60, 159–160
special visitor services: 20
spring visits: hiking 132–133; weather conditions 8–9, 16
squirrels: 38, 39, 40, 43, 112, 124
star-gazing activities: 34
state parks: 28
St. George, Utah: 88
St. Louis, Missouri, distance from: 3
strenuous hikes: 138–139
summer visits: backcountry regions 118; weather conditions 8–9, 16
sunrises/sunsets: 35
sunscreen/sunglasses: 16, 131, 132
Sunset Crater National Monument: 27, 157
Supai: 36–37, 139, 146
Supai Tunnel: 22, 70, 83, 137
swimming: 129

T

tassel-eared squirrels: 38
taxi service: 69

telephone directory: 198–203
temperatures: 8–9, 16, 28, 132–133
Ten-X Campground: 110
three-day visits: 79
Three-Mile rest house: 64, 137
Thunderbird Lodge: 11, 91
thunderstorms: 8–9, 16
toads: 38
toilets: 13, 204
Tonto Platform: 82
Toroweap Valley: 47, 169
tours: see bus tours; guided trips; ranger-led walks and programs
towing services: 204
Trailer Village: 11, 17, 93, 108–109
trails: see hiking
Trailview Overlook: 69, 72
train service: 6, 65, 163, 165, 172, 182
trans-canyon shuttle service: 6, 12, 76
Transept Trail: 21, 86, 135
Transportation Desks: 25
transportation services: 198–199; see also specific service
transportation tips: 68–71
trash: see waste disposal
travelers checks: 205
trees: 51
tribal lands: 28
Tuckup Trail: 123
Tucson, Arizona, distance from: 3
Tusayan: food/restaurants 101; lodging 94–95; visitor services 4, 11
Tusayan Museum and Ruins: general discussion 24; bookstore 11; family activities 176; ranger-led walks and programs 80, 114; self-guided walking tours 57–58, 84; sightseeing tips 20
Tuweep: 123
Tuweep Campground: 17, 123
Tuzigoot Ruin National Monument: 157
two-day visits: 78

U

Uncle Jim's Point: 70, 83
Uncle Jim Trail: 21–22, 52, 86, 137
Underwood, Gilbert Stanley: 81, 92

Unkar Creek: 59
Unkar Delta: 59
uranium mines: 170
U.S. Army: 64
Utah deervetch: 52–53

V

Valle, Arizona: 95
vegetation: 26–27, 49–53, 119
Verkamp, John: 63, 84, 166
Verkamp, Michael: 63
Verkamp's Curios: 12, 63, 84
Vermilion Cliffs National Monument: 27, 76, 172
viewing tips: animal population 40–41; area attractions 156–157; birds 46–48; one-day visitors 20–22; park attractions 176–177, 198; three-day visits 79; transportation choices 68–71; two-day visits 78; waterfalls 36–37
Village Route: 68, 72–73
Vishnu schist: 29
visitor centers: 12, 23–25
visitor facilities and services: 11–13, 23–25, 203, 204–206
visitors with disabilities: 7, 72–73, 206
Vista Encantada: 75
volcanic activity: 29–30

WXYZ

wagon rides: 146
Walhalla Glades Ruin: 58, 85
Walhalla Overlook: 58, 75
Walhalla Plateau: 166
walking trails: 68, 128
Walnut Canyon National Monument: 27, 157
waste disposal: 112, 121, 133
Watchtower: 55, 170, 181
waterfalls: guided trips 147; moderate hikes 137; mule trips 70, 83; sightseeing tips 36–37; strenuous hikes 139

water supply: 169, 171
weather conditions: 4–5, 8–9, 10, 16, 118
western Grand Canyon: hiking 139; horseback riding 146–147
western spotted skunk: 39
West Rim Drive: *see* Hermit Road
wheelchairs: 72–73, 206
Whistle Stop Cafe: 103
white-tailed antelope: 39
white-water rafting: 129, 142–144, 185–187
Whittlesey, Charles: 63, 81
Widforss, Gunnar: 84
Widforss Point: 22, 86
Widforss Trail: 22, 52, 85, 137
wilderness areas: *see* backcountry regions
wilderness permits: 24, 25
wildfires: 171
wildflowers: 49–50, 52–53
wildlife population: 26–27, 38–43, 119, 124–125
wild turkeys: 39, 47
Williams, Arizona: bus service 5–6; driving distances 2; entrance points 4; food/restaurants 101–102; lodging 95–96; train service 6, 65, 163, 165
Wilson, Francis: 63, 81
Winslow, Arizona, distance from: 2
winter visits: general discussion 88; backcountry regions 118; recreational opportunities 150–151; weather conditions 8–9, 16
World Heritage Site: 171
Wotan's Throne: 166
Wupatki National Monument: 27, 157
Xanterra Parks and Resorts: 14, 15
Yaki Point: 68, 72, 75
Yavapai Lodge: 11, 91–92, 99–100
Yavapai Observation Station: easy hikes 135; shuttle services 68, 72; sightseeing tips 20; visitor services 11, 23
Zion National Park: 3, 27

· Acknowledgments ·

"It seems a gigantic statement even for nature to make."
—John Muir, in *Steep Trails*

We are indebted to Jack O'Brien and Josh Englander for their invaluable help in developing and editing the manuscript; Stacy Frank for her careful research and editing for the revised edition; Frank Ansley for his help in updating illustrations; Chuck Wahler for his careful review and edit of the material; Research Librarian Sara T. Stebbins, Museum Curator Carolyn Richard and Archivist Colleen Hyde at Grand Canyon National Park for their generous assistance with photo research and resource materials; Pam Frazier and the staff of the Grand Canyon Association for their help in locating resource materials; Tom and Mona Mesereau at Amfac Parks & Resorts and David Whiteside and the Grand Canyon Trust for their help with research; Mary Delle Gunn at the Grand Canyon National Park Foundation and the National Park Service staff at Grand Canyon, especially Maureen Oltrogge, Sandy Pearl, Ellen Sealy, Laura Douris, Stu Fritz, Lynn Picard, Mike Hoffman, Brian Wisher, Susan Lakes, and Jim Tuck for their help in making this guidebook as accurate as possible. Thanks also to Janet Dean and Pam McCosker for their invaluable help in researching, editing, and assembling the original information. We would also like to thank Grace Fujimoto of Avalon Travel for her invaluable help in making this new edition possible.

SUSAN AND PHIL FRANK

Susan Frank spent many of her childhood weekends camping in the Sierra Nevada and fishing California rivers and lakes with her family. She saw her first grizzly bear on the Katmai Peninsula in Alaska at age ten and spent more enjoyable hours waiting for fish to bite her line than actually catching them. After earning a degree in European history from the University of California, Berkeley, she taught in Minnesota and California before starting a career in communications. In 1990, she founded a media and marketing consulting company, working with a variety of clients throughout the San Francisco Bay Area.

Cartoonist Phil Frank's daily cartoon strip *Farley* kept a finger on the pulse of the San Francisco Bay Area for more than 21 years, ever since Phil decided to move the strip from national syndication to focus his considerable talents on issues closer to home. The strip was dearly loved and followed daily by a local cadre of fans. Indeed, *Farley* became one of San Francisco's most recognized and reliable landmarks. In 2004, Phil started a nationally syndicated strip with writer Joe Troise called *Elderberries*, which turned a humorous eye to the issues of aging in America. Phil passed away in September of 2007, but his *Elderberries* strip still runs in newspapers across the country.

Susan and Phil started their life together on a houseboat in Sausalito, California. This led to their first book collaboration, a children's book about living on the water. Both avid history buffs, they moved from ship to shore about 10 years ago. Susan lives in Sausalito in a 1914 Craftsman-style home, from which she ventures into California's national parks and other wilderness areas in search of inspiration for new books. Her family includes two grown children, three grandchildren, and Gus, a feisty Cairn Terrier.